BORN *to* ORGANIZE

Sara Pedersen

Please note that the information in this book is intended for the novice professional organizer and should be used only as a general guide. For more in-depth information about any business aspects (such as liability insurance, business entity decisions, tax or financial questions, or legal issues), please contact your attorney or tax accountant. The author disclaims any liability for any damages, losses, or injuries that may result from the use or misuse of any advice, information, or product recommendations presented in this book.

ISBN-13: 978-0-9786733-4-5
ISBN-10: 0-9786733-4-4
Updated 1117

table of contents

MARKETING YOUR BUSINESS

APPENDIX A

APPENDIX B

APPENDIX C

APPENDIX D

CONCLUSION

exploring professional organizing as a career

what makes a great professional organizer?

As a professional organizer and small business owner, you'll need:

THE LOVE OF ALL THINGS "ORGANIZING"
Maybe you weren't born organized, but if you're seriously considering a career as a professional organizer, then you were probably born to organize! It's definitely a calling, a passion, and a mission for thousands of people in this industry. We can't get enough of it — the great organizing products, the excitement when we see a cluttered and chaotic space become clear and peaceful, and the desire to share our knowledge with others. We simply love to organize. Make sure you do too!

THE ABILITY TO TEACH
You must really enjoy helping people. When you are organizing, it is not about you. It's all about the client. Many people say they've been organized all their lives, but that doesn't always translate into being a fantastic professional organizer. It's one thing to organize for yourself. It's another to transfer your skills to other people based on their needs, lifestyles, and learning styles. If you enjoy sharing your organizing knowledge, you'll truly help your clients, and they'll be happy and satisfied.

THE ABILITY TO SEE THINGS FROM YOUR CLIENTS' PERSPECTIVES
Sure, you love to organize stuff. It comes naturally for you. But for most of your clients, it's neither natural nor fun. So you'll need to take the time to get to know them, why they are disorganized, what organizing techniques and products they've tried in the past, and what they expect from you. What does organizing success look like to them? Maybe they're not shooting for perfection, but something as simple as getting out the door on time each morning.

THE ABILITY TO WEAR MANY HATS
Unless your small business is really up and coming, you won't have the staff to handle the day-to-day administrative tasks. So you'll need to set aside time on your calendar for things like bookkeeping, marketing, supply shopping, and database management. Once you can afford it, you could hire someone to help with the jobs you don't enjoy or aren't good at. But in the early months (and even years), you'll be doing a bit of everything.

THE ABILITY TO EMBRACE SUCCESS AND LEARN FROM MISTAKES
Success can come in many forms — reaching your income goals for the year, landing a choice client, getting interviewed on television, or simply helping a client master a new skill. Failure can appear in just as many ways — difficulty finding new clients, not being able to help a client "get it," or missing a deadline. While the failures can stand out, realize that most likely only you are seeing them. Learn from your mistakes and embrace your successes.

Excited to learn more and begin your journey to a career as a professional organizer? Just turn the page...

defining a professional organizer

Professional organizers are trained and skilled individuals who coach their clients to develop new systems to improve various aspects of their lives. According to the National Association of Productivity and Organizing Professionals (NAPO), professional organizers "support evaluation, decision-making, and action around objects, space, and data; helping clients achieve desired outcomes regarding function, order, and clarity." Professional organizers teach clients "the skills they need to solve a lifetime of organizing problems by designing systems and processes using established organizing principles."

With the help of a professional organizer, clients can accomplish more at work or home; meet deadlines; find things faster; gain control of their surroundings; reduce clutter; improve their quality of life; create streamlined processes; and much more. A professional organizer is an educator, trainer, coach, or consultant, not a cleaning person. (Organizing focuses on people while cleaning focuses on objects.) If, as a professional organizer, you are tidying up a space without transferring skills or knowledge to the client, then you will not command as high a rate.

As a professional organizer, you must be compassionate, not judgmental, toward clients. Although you must be a detail-oriented person, you must also be flexible enough to make changes on the fly. Professional organizers tailor solutions for each client. They don't impose one-size-fits-all answers. You must also have great listening skills. You need to be able to really hear your clients. You must not only ask the right questions to get to the root of their organizing problems but also listen to their answers. (And often read between the lines.) Keep an open mind with your clients, and make suggestions. But always let them know that they're the boss; they get final say over your suggested solutions.

skill building

It's important to gain practice in helping others get organized. Get unpaid experience by organizing for family, friends, coworkers, or a local charity. Ask them to write letters of recommendation or "kudos" for you to use on your website or to have on hand when potential clients ask for references. Take "before and after" photos for your portfolio.

Learn from the pros by searching out an apprenticeship or mentorship. If you can find an experienced professional organizer in your area who needs an extra set of hands during larger jobs, offer yours for free. You'll gain valuable insight into the industry and hone your skills. Consider this an unpaid internship. Or, consider hiring a mentor or coach to guide you through the first few months or years. Consider this part of your educational expenses. The money you spend will pay off quickly, as you get immediate answers to your specific questions, much-needed accountability, and a new colleague and friend in the organizing industry.

educational resources

RECOMMENDED ORGANIZING BOOKS

- *ADD-Friendly Ways to Organize Your Life* by Judith Kolberg
  (It's a fabulous resource for both you and your ADD clients.)

- *Buried in Treasures* by David Tolin
  (A great guide to educate you on compulsive acquiring, saving, and hoarding.)

- *Clear Your Clutter with Feng Shui* by Karen Kingston
  (Even if you're not into feng shui, it's a fabulous quick-read resource.)

- *Conquering Chronic Disorganization* by Judith Kolberg
  (It explains CD and how to help clients with it.)

- *Don't Toss My Memories in the Trash* by Vickie Dellaquila
  (A step-by-step guide to helping seniors downsize, organize, and move.)

- *The ICD Guide to Challenging Disorganization: For Professional Organizers*
  by the Institute for Challenging Disorganization and edited by Kate Varness
  (A step-by-step guide to helping CD clients.)

- *It's All Too Much, Does This Clutter Make My Butt Look Fat?* and
  Enough Already! by Peter Walsh
  (These three books share Peter's system for letting go of physical and emotional clutter.)

- *The Organized Student* by Donna Goldberg
  (If you work with students, you must read this book.)

- *Organizing from the Inside Out* and *Time Management from the Inside Out*
  by Julie Morgenstern
  (Essential reading. These two are must-buy books.)

- *Organizing from the Right Side of the Brain* by Lee Silber
  (Great organizing strategies for creative folks, those with ADD, and anyone looking for "outside the box" organizational ideas.)

- *Organizing the Disorganized Child* by Martin L. Kutscher and Marcella Moran
  (Essential reading if you'll be working with children from elementary through high school.)

- *The Life-Changing Magic of Tidying Up* by Marie Kondo
  (This best-selling book guides readers to find items that "spark joy" and discard the rest.)

MAGAZINES: GREAT SOURCES OF ORGANIZING TIPS AND INFORMATION

- *Real Simple* (a must-have for professional organizers)
- *Martha Stewart Living* (many creative organizing tips)
- *Entrepreneur* and *Inc.* (both devoted to small-business owners and entrepreneurs)

Also frequently helpful are:

- *Better Homes and Gardens*
- *Family Circle*
- *Good Housekeeping*
- *HGTV Magazine*
- *Woman's Day*

TIP: Take a field trip to your local library to peruse the recommended books and magazines listed above. It's nice to "try before you buy!" If any of the publications wow you, you can then purchase them at your local bookstore or Amazon. If you discover any brilliant magazine articles, make a copy of them and start an "idea file" for organizing inspiration.

WEBSITES RELATED TO ORGANIZING AND ASSOCIATED ISSUES

- Association of Closet and Storage Professionals: www.closets.org
- Attention Deficit Disorder Association: www.add.org
- Board of Certification for Professional Organizers: www.certifiedprofessionalorganizers.org
- Children and Adults with Attention Deficit Disorder: www.chadd.org
- Clutterers Anonymous: www.clutterersanonymous.net
- Faithful Organizers: www.faithfulorganizers.com
- Institute for Challenging Disorganization: www.challengingdisorganization.org
- International Association of Home Staging Professionals: www.iahsp.com
- International Coach Federation: www.coachfederation.org
- International OCD Foundation: www.ocfoundation.org
- National Association of Productivity and Organizing Professionals: www.napo.net
- National Association of Senior Move Managers: www.nasmm.org
- Professional Organizers in Canada: www.organizersincanada.com

WEBSITES ESPECIALLY FOR PROFESSIONAL ORGANIZERS OUTSIDE OF THE U.S. AND CANADA

- Africa: Professional Organiser Association Africa: poaa.wordpress.com
- Australia, New Zealand, Singapore, and Hong Kong: Australasian Association of Professional Organisers: www.aapo.org.au
- Brazil: ANPOP: www.anpop.com.br
- Finland: Professional Organizers in Finland: www.ammattijarjestajat.fi
- Germany: Büroordnung Büroorganisation Netzwerk Deutschland: www.boond.de
- Japan: Japan Association of Life Organizers: www.jalo.jp
- Republic of Korea: The Korea Association of Professional Organizers: www.kapo100.org
- Netherlands: Dutch Association of Professional Organizers: www.nbpo.nl
- the UK: Association of Professional Declutterers and Organisers UK: www.apdo-uk.co.uk

CLASSES
Consider your education level. While a college education is certainly not required, nor a perfect gauge of an organizer's success, it — along with prior work experiences in various fields — can be helpful.

Attend local workshops on organizing. (Try community education classes.) No matter how long you've been organizing, there is always room to learn new organizing techniques. Never stop learning. And yes, it's okay to take classes taught by another professional organizer. We all have our own techniques and can learn from one another. But be respectful of the instructor. This is her class, so don't pipe in with your own ideas or steal her thunder. Feel free to introduce yourself in private and let her know how much you enjoyed the class. You may make a new friend!

And take NAPO's live webinars and on-demand courses. Some include: Starting an Organizing Business, Fundamental Organizing and Productivity Skills, Starting Out as a Residential Organizer, Starting Out as a Business Organizer, Chronic Disorganization, Project Management for Professional Organizers, and Transference of Organizing Skills. There is a fee for them (ranging from $45 - $299, with members getting discounted prices), but you'll find them very helpful, especially if you don't have any other education opportunities in your area. These will be helpful to you throughout your organizing career, whether you're in the newbie stage or are a veteran organizer. Keep learning! Register at www.napo.net.

certification

NAPO developed a certification program for professional organizers in 2007 that is operated by the Board of Certification for Professional Organizers® (BCPO®). Certification is certainly not required to become an organizer, nor is it currently expected or even attainable to new organizers. (You must have 1,500 hours of paid work experience in the last three years to qualify to sit for the exam.) But as an established professional organizer, certification will certainly lend credibility. Once certified, you'll be able to list the title of Certified Professional Organizer® after your name. You'll be in an elite group and will have a great selling point thanks to your certification. View eligibility requirements, recommended reading, and more at www.certifiedprofessionalorganizers.org.

joining NAPO

One thing you can do right away to boost your credibility is to join NAPO. You can become a member at any point, whether you have experience or not. Membership with NAPO is well worth the $275 annual dues. It has a great online member directory so prospects can find you based on location or speciality. It has an educational e-newsletter, online discussion groups, and special interest groups. The networking and volunteer opportunities are fabulous. And, as a member, you may purchase its professional organizer's liability insurance plan. Throw in the educational webinars and the national conference (both have additional charges, but are well worth the money), and you won't want to miss out on these benefits. Note that members begin with a "provisional" status, which includes all the membership perks except being part of the online "find an organizer" directory. Members can advance to "professional" status once the three courses in NAPO's Professional Practices Curriculum are completed via webinar.

You should also consider joining your local chapter of NAPO, if available. You'll be thrilled to learn that most of the other organizers won't view you as "the competition" and are generous in sharing their experiences and knowledge with you. The benefits you'll receive will far outweigh the dues you'll pay. In addition to the opportunity to form friendships and business relationships with fellow members, you'll receive on-going education at the chapter programs. You'll form alliances with people in related and complementary fields, such as closet installation or office supply companies. Local chapters offer great opportunities for learning new skills and sharing your expertise through volunteering on their board of directors and chapter committees. And, importantly, you'll receive exposure through your chapter's website, which most likely lists a member roster. And that's how many of your clients might find you.

pros and cons of professional organizing

The pros of being a professional organizer greatly outweigh any cons. Before you "take the leap," make a list of positives and negatives. Here are some ideas to get you started.

PROS

- be your own boss
- set your own hours
- use your talents and skills
- help others
- meet others like you
- people need your services
- see immediate results after each client visit
- feel good about improving someone's life
- use your creativity
- low start-up costs
- opportunity to specialize in many different areas of organizing (residential, office, working with seniors, kids or moms, speaking or coaching, writing books, etc.)

CONS

- lack of steady, dependable income
- sometimes working in dirty conditions
- some clients will be difficult to help
- you must "do it all" (balance the books, create marketing strategies, buy supplies
- you will not receive traditional fringe benefits, such as a retirement plan, vacation or sick pay, or medical insurance

---

TIP: Make note of what you loved most about your past jobs. Can you continue some of those aspects in a career as a professional organizer? What did you like least? Will professional organizing allow you to avoid some of those things?

---

organizing specialties

Professional organizing has many specialties. You don't have to commit to one particular area right off the bat, but it's ideal to specialize at some point. You'll find it much easier to market your services once you have a niche, so try to eventually narrow down your services offered and audience served. Rather than being a Jack (or Jill) of all trades, try to select an area (or two) in which you truly excel and shine. Make that your niche, learn all you can, and become "the expert" in your town. Then, offer other organizing services that complement and enhance your niche. Some include:

HOME (RESIDENTIAL) ORGANIZING

- closet organizing and/or design and installation
- garages, attics, and basements
- home office
- photos, memorabilia, and collections
- whole-house decluttering and organizing

OFFICE ORGANIZING

- commercial office
- home office
- medical or legal office
- storage/warehouse
- electronic organization
- ergonomics
- financial/bookkeeping
- inventory/asset control
- paper management
- time management

WORKING WITH SPECIAL SEGMENTS OF THE POPULATION

- children or students
- the chronically disorganized
- families or busy moms and dads
- hoarders
- people with disabilities
- seniors/downsizers
- those who have ADD/ADHD

OTHER UNIQUE NICHES

- estate organizing
- errands, personal shopping, image consulting
- feng shui
- garage & estate sales
- green organizing
- group trainer
- interior design, redesign, and staging
- meeting and event coordination
- moving and relocation assistance

- personal or life coaching
- public speaking or product spokesperson
- space planning
- writing

What intrigues you the most? Start there. But don't close the door on other opportunities. You may find that an area you hadn't considered turns out to be your favorite type of job!

Once you've been working with clients for a few months, take some time to figure out what you like and do best. Ask yourself, "What type of organizing have I enjoyed the most, and what have I disliked the most?" What client types are you most motivated to work with? Do you have clients that you can hardly wait to see again? What is it about them that you love? These should be your target market! You'll easily discover your niche once you can pinpoint what (and who) you most love to organize.

time commitment expectations

Each day is unique and full of challenges and wonderful rewards. Some days are downright exciting — like when you transform a room from chaotic into calm, serene, and functional. Some days are kind of boring — like when you need to prepare your taxes, run errands for office supplies, or update your database. Like any other job, professional organizing will have its ups and downs.

Some organizers work full-time, which includes billable client hours plus non-billable time spent running the business. Others work part-time. Be aware that in order to work full-time, you'll need to build your client list, which can take a while. You may need to work for another established professional organizer (sub-contracting) or pay for referrals from another organizer if you want billable hours.

TIP: A word on working another job while you get your organizing business up and running. The majority of professional organizers make organizing their primary career. That being said, sometimes it's just financially necessary to work elsewhere just to keep a steady paycheck and benefits until your client base is established. There's nothing wrong with that! Many organizers who worked their "day jobs," and organized in the evenings and on weekends until their client bases were large enough to support them. Many work part-time hours during the week so they can see clients during daytime hours. Just don't burn yourself out. Organizing can be tiring, and you need to be at full strength for your clients.

No matter how many hours you work with clients, don't forget to plan for administrative business time. You'll most likely be doing all the work yourself — from running errands to returning client phone calls, to working on marketing strategies, to managing your database. It may be helpful to set aside a certain time each day or certain days of the week just for administrative work. What you put into it is what you get out of it! Being self-employed takes lots of time and energy to get underway.

Some non-client tasks you'll need to find time for include:

- marketing your business
- purchasing supplies
- creating and updating your database
- financial record-keeping
- doing yearly or quarterly taxes
- prep time for client sessions (researching their special needs for products, gathering information on special organizing projects that you haven't yet experienced)
- reading, studying, and researching to stay current and to continue your organizer's education

Some days you may have a couple client sessions, and some days you'll have none. Take advantage of those non-client days to catch up on administrative tasks and market your business to the max so you can fill those appointment slots with paying jobs. Conversely, if your schedule is filling up with client sessions, you might consider spending your time doing what you do best and outsource the rest.

TIP: If your administrative chores are getting in the way, it may be time to enlist help. Hire an assistant or outsource some of the work, such as bookkeeping, marketing, or other essential (but time-consuming) tasks. It may be hard to pay someone else to do this work, but think of the money you could be making if you simply had the extra time! Consider hiring a local high school or college student for simple jobs, or ask colleagues for a referral to qualified professionals in your area. Another option is to hire a Virtual Assistant (VA) who can help you via email and phone with administrative, creative, and technical services. The International Virtual Assistants Association (IVAA) has a helpful website where you can learn more and locate a qualified VA. Details at www.ivaa.org.

---

getting your business in order

Now that you've learned a bit about the field of professional organizing, it's time to get your business in order. This section will guide you through start-up costs, record-keeping, insurance, setting your fees, business name and entity considerations, and more.

start-up costs

One nice thing about this career is that start-up costs are low. You won't need a lot of money to get going.

Most organizers work out of their home offices. Unless you're at the point where you have a staff, renting office space is a huge waste of money. But making the best use of your space is important. You'll work more effectively if you create a space that's both functional and beautiful. If noise and distractions are a concern, find a secluded spot. Any spare room where you can shut the door — bedroom, attic, or basement — is great.

TIP: Make sure to have good lighting, both indirect and direct. Invest in comfortable office furniture. (If you find a traditional office chair uncomfortable, consider replacing it with a yoga ball!) Take the time to add a little "you" to the room. Paint the walls a color you love. Add artwork — whether expensive originals or a child's framed finger paintings. Energize yourself with your favorite music. Then add a little greenery in the form of a potted plant or fresh flowers.

Your home office will also need a computer, printer, and reliable internet access. In addition to basic word processing software, you may also want to invest in accounting software (such as QuickBooks, Quicken, or FreshBooks) and a database or contact management program (sometimes called a CRM), such as Access, FileMaker Pro, Act!, or Salesforce. You could even use a simple program like Excel to act as your bookkeeping and/or database management program.

You'll need to buy some office and "in the field" supplies. (See list in the "Preparing Your Take-Along Bag" section.) You'll need a phone line with voicemail. (A cell phone works nicely.) A smartphone is all you need to capture great "before and after" photos. You may want to purchase a PO box to receive your mail, allowing your home address to retain anonymity, although it's not a necessity.

You'll need to set aside some funds for your business entity filing (see the "Choosing a Business Entity" section) and, importantly, business liability insurance.

For your start-up marketing, hire a graphic designer to create a fabulous company logo and simple-yet-stunning business cards, and develop a professional-looking website. As your business grows, invest some earnings back into your business marketing efforts.

Once you get the initial start-up equipment in place and some income flowing into your bank account, your next business expense may be membership dues for the National Association of Productivity and Organizing Professionals (NAPO) and/or a local networking group. Recognize that although the dues may seem expensive, you should consider them an investment in yourself and your business. Additional marketing efforts, such as sending direct mail campaigns, will also help your business grow.

It's wise to keep your business checking account separate from your personal bank account, so call a few local banks to inquire about their small business packages. You will likely be able to find one with no monthly fees. Having a separate credit card for business expenses can be helpful as well. Find one with no annual fee and pay it off in full each month if possible. (Some offer organizer-relevant cash-back incentives, such as for purchases made at office supply stores!)

record-keeping

From the very beginning, be sure to track your expenses and revenues carefully. Use a spreadsheet program like Excel or a small business financial software program like QuickBooks, Quicken, or FreshBooks. If you're not good with numbers, it may be in your best interest to hire an accountant or bookkeeper to help with this aspect of your business.

Whether you hire an accountant to do your taxes or you're the do-it-yourself type, it's important to understand the multitude of deductible business expenses available to the small business owner. Some expense categories for a professional organizer may include the following, but consult an accountant for a complete list of deductible expenses unique to your business.

- advertising (printing marketing materials, Google AdWords, print advertisements, etc.)
- car expenses (mileage OR repair expense if used exclusively for business purposes)
- dues for professional organizations (like NAPO, POC, or ICD)
- gifts for clients up to a max of $25 per person
- educational materials and classes specific to your job (books and magazines on organizing, webinars, teleclasses, conference fees)
- home office (may include a portion of utilities)
- internet services, business phone expenses, web site hosting and domain names
- insurance for your business
- interest and fees on business-only credit cards, bank service charges
- legal and professional services (accountant, lawyer, marketing consultant, etc.)
- office expenses, small equipment, and furnishings
- supplies
- taxes and licenses
- travel and meals related to business

TIP: Be sure to save receipts for all purchases. Highlight the date, price, and type of product/ service on each receipt. You can file them in an expandable wallet folder, or group them by month or type of expense in separate envelopes. Or go paperless by scanning them with a product like NeatReceipts. There are many ways to store receipts, and you'll need to determine which method works best for you. The most important thing is to have a system so everything stays organized throughout the year. You might check out some of the newest apps that allow you track your business expenses right from your smartphone or tablet.

If you have a separate space within your home that you use solely for business purposes (your home office), you may want to investigate the home office deduction. It can be a great money-saver. And when you claim the home office deduction, you can claim the miles driven from your home to a client's or other business-related stop. (If you don't claim your office as a deduction, you cannot claim business miles starting at your home as that is considered "commute" miles.) Remember that you need to formally track your business mileage in a log book or a computer program like Excel or QuickBooks. Or consider one of the easy-to-use apps for your smartphone. Search for "mileage log" to find apps that can automatically calculate your mileage using GPS technology!

When in doubt, consult an accountant for full details. Even if you do your own taxes each year, it might be worthwhile to schedule a consultation with a CPA to make sure you're maximizing all potential deductions.

insurance

Seriously consider purchasing business insurance, which can provide coverage for your business property and liability. Yes, you need it! Contact insurance agents in your area to find a policy that suits you. Make sure you give detailed information about the type of services you provide so that the policy will cover you fully. For example, you'll want to be covered if you (or a client) get hurt during or as a result of an organizing session, or if you accidentally break something. Also, you'll want to be covered in case a client accuses you of stealing or destroying his/her property. Take the time to fully discuss your needs with your agent, including a conversation about professional liability coverage (also called errors and omissions coverage), which can protect against a professional negligence claim.

In addition to business liability insurance, be sure to contact your current homeowner's insurance agency, letting them know about your new business venture. Likely, your home office supplies and equipment are covered under your homeowner's policy, but it's best to check.

Wondering about bonding? It's different from insurance. A bond is a financial guarantee that you will honor a business contract in a timely, satisfactory manner. If the contractor fails to meet the guidelines, the bonding company will pay the client for the services. If you don't meet the guidelines, then you — the contractor — will have to contend with the bonding company. A bond is not an insurance policy. If you're unsure if you need to be bonded in your state, check with your Secretary of State's office. (Bonding is quite uncommon in the professional organizing field, so you probably don't need it, but each situation is unique, so check to be sure.)

In addition to having business insurance, follow these common-sense tactics to keep your business safe:

- Take caution if you decide to remove items from your clients' homes at their request (such as hauling away clothing and furniture donations). Make sure your clients do all the loading of items into your vehicle. You wouldn't want to be liable for removing items that were not supposed to leave the premises.

- Along the same line, as you're sorting through items in clients' homes (especially paperwork), make sure to put the trash/recycling bins or shredder near the clients and have them take charge of disposal — relieving you of liability if they accuse you of tossing something of value.

- Consider always having clients on-site with you. That way, there is minimal chance they could accuse you of theft, as they were with you the entire time.

- Be careful about providing advice outside your area of expertise. Financial questions should be referred to a financial planner or accountant, legal questions to a lawyer, and so on. You are a professional organizer, not a CPA, attorney, doctor, or therapist. Know your boundaries.

setting your fee

Now comes the fun part — setting your rates. Because you're being paid to teach, coach, and/or consult, you'll be making (and deserve) a fabulous hourly rate. But often, new organizers don't feel comfortable charging enough for their services! As you set your fee, remember these things:

- There are some industry standards, but they vary widely (see next paragraph).

- Rates tend to vary by region and type of organizing (residential vs. business).

- Professional organizers with more experience charge more than those with little to none.

- Even though you may have little to no experience, you still have so much to share with your clients. Yes, you are worth the fee you charge, but if you don't believe it, neither will your prospects and clients.

TIP: According to the 2009 NAPO Member Survey, 81% of respondents use a "by the hour" pricing structure most of the time, while 6% bill on a per-project basis, and 10% use packaged services. For those that price by the hour, a rate between $40 to over $200 an hour is the norm.

SALARY SCENARIOS

It's really simple to figure out a few salary scenarios. First, determine what you want to make annually, and then work backward to figure out how much you'll need to work weekly to attain that goal. This will help you figure out how much to charge per hour. Remember, these are the "billable hours" you'll work. This does not include the non-billable hours, such as doing administrative and marketing tasks. You don't get paid for those! Also, please note that these examples represent gross revenue. Remember, you'll be paying taxes at the end of the year.

In these scenarios, let's say you'll be working 50 weeks out of the year.

If you want to make $22,500 per year:
$22,500 divided by 50 weeks per year = $450 per week
Now, how many billable hours can you work per week?
If you will work 10 billable hours per week, then you'll need to charge $45 per hour.
If you will work only 6 billable hours per week, then you'll need to charge $75 per hour.

Let's try it with a few other scenarios:

If you want to make $50,000 per year:
$50,000 divided by 50 weeks per year = $1000 per week
If you will work 20 billable hours per week, then you'll need to charge $50 per hour.
If you will work only 10 billable hours per week, then you'll need to charge $100 per hour.

If you want to make $100,000 per year:
$100,000 divided by 50 weeks per year = $2000 per week
If you will work 20 billable hours per week, then you'll need to charge $100 per hour.
If you will work only 10 billable hours per week, then you'll need to charge $200 per hour.

Have a goal so you have something to reach for, but try to be realistic about the hours you can work and the clients you can find. The early months and years can sometimes be a struggle to find the client base you desire, and it's unlikely you'll maintain a constant number of work hours throughout the year. But everything is possible! In addition to the time spent on administrative and marketing tasks, you'll need time to educate yourself on new organizing techniques and products. You don't get paid for these non-billable hours. The figure scenarios above do not factor in vacation time, sick days, and cancellations.

TIP: Note that you'll be reinvesting much of your income back into your business, especially during the first couple years. Start-ups often spend 80% of the first year's income on marketing expenses. Remember that you'll have to spend some money to make money!

PACKAGE AND PROJECT PRICING

Although most professional organizers charge by the hour, there are other pricing options to consider. Some organizers offer a discount package when a certain number of hours is purchased in advance. For example, "Buy 9 hours and the 10th is free," or, "Fifteen percent off a package of 30 hours." The nice thing about this is that you get the money upfront and don't have the hassle of collecting payment at the end of each session.

Many organizers have a flat-rate session fee, such as a half-day or full-day session. Additionally, some organizers have a flat-rate fee for specific projects, such as an executive's office or desktop de-cluttering session. Bidding jobs on a project basis can be tricky, especially for new organizers. But for some veteran organizers, it's the best way to go. You'll receive full payment upfront, and the client commits to organizing until the job is done. The benefit to flat-rate pricing (also called project pricing) is that the client can stop watching the clock during sessions and focus fully on the job at hand. However, learning to accurately gauge project time often takes years. And even then, it's still difficult! After the payment has been made, the financial risk is taken off the client and put onto you, with hopes that the project takes the amount of time you've estimated.

TRAVEL TIME

Don't forget to consider travel time and car expenses as you set your rate. Decide upfront how far you're willing to travel for clients. (For some, this may be just "in town." For others, it may be 15, 30, or even 60 miles.) It is not advantageous to charge a separate travel fee for clients unless you need to go an extraordinary distance. Most clients who live outside a major metro area, or those with no other professional organizers in their area, are likely to consider travel expenses as an inherent part of their fee.

UNDERSTAND YOUR VALUE

What if a client has a tight budget? In some cases, clients really cannot afford your services at full price. In these cases, you have a few options. You might set aside a certain number of hours each month or year to do pro bono work for truly needy and motivated people. Volunteering for a great cause brings good karma! It's also a wonderful way to get your name and face in front of local charities, and if you spin it right, you might be able to get some awesome PR in your local paper or on the evening news. At the very least, ask for a written testimonial and take before and after photos. Just remember to set a limit on the amount of pro bono work you offer each year so you don't get burnt out. Or, offer them other options, such as working with you for a limited number of hours at full price, but offering them "homework" so they can work between sessions on their own. Or direct them to some great organizing books and online resources.

Most of all, realize that we tend to value things that we pay for more than the stuff we get for free. There is a perceived value to things for which we pay good money. Very often clients think they can't afford to hire a professional organizer, yet they are coming home daily with bags of junk they just bought but really don't need. Let them know that hiring you is an investment in their life. If you experience a client balking at your prices, it's a good opportunity to eloquently and efficiently explain the value of your services. To do so:

- Figure out your clients' "pain," such as what is driving them most crazy, and what "success" looks like to them.

- Tell them how you can provide solutions to fix what ails them (and their home/office).

- Share with them the benefits of being organized that go beyond a neat and tidy home/ office (such as less stress, more time to do what's important to them, being more productive, having a better self-image, etc.)

If you ever feel that you're not worth the amount of money you're charging, consider this story excerpted from *Selling the Invisible: A Field Guide to Modern Marketing* by Harry Beckwith. This book is essential reading for anyone selling a service, including professional organizers. It includes sections on surveying and research, marketing, how prospects think, positioning, focus, pricing, communicating and selling, and nurturing and keeping clients. It also includes an especially good section on branding your business, which is imperative if you want to distinguish yourself from your competition.

A man was suffering a persistent problem with his house. The floor squeaked. No matter what he tried, nothing worked. Finally, he called a carpenter who friends said was a true craftsman. The craftsman walked into the room and heard the squeak. He set down his toolbox, pulled out a hammer and nail, and pounded the nail into the floor with three blows. The squeak was gone forever. The carpenter pulled out an invoice slip, on which he wrote the total of $45.

Above the total were two line items:
Hammering: $2
Knowing where to hammer: $43

Charge for knowing where.

Also, even though you may have no experience as a professional organizer, remember your prior work experiences. Everything you've done up until this point is some type of work experience. Incorporate all the things you have to offer as you set your fee.

TIP: There are pros and cons to posting your rates on your website. Some professional organizers argue that if you post your rates, you'll weed out those who don't want to pay your fee, saving you time. (There are people who will always choose the lowest-priced service provider, rather than focusing on expertise, qualifications, and ability.) However, you'll also miss out on the opportunity to share the true value and benefits they'd receive if they hired you. A website can't do that the way a one-on-one interaction — a phone conversation or in-person meeting — can. Not posting them also gives you the flexibility to increase your rates for special circumstances and as your comfort level, experience, and client base increase. On the pro side to posting your rates, many prospects appreciate knowing up front what you charge. And if your rates are on the lower end of the scale, then you may appear more attractive to them compared to others with higher rates.

---

other income sources

Hands-on, in-person organizing may be your "bread and butter," but consider some other sources to supplement your income, and give you (and your aching body) a break:

OFFER IN-HOME CLASSES FOR GROUPS
Each person can kick in a set amount (say $25), which is a minimum investment to learn directly from a professional organizer. But when 10 people get together, you'll make $250. (Added incentive: You might let the host attend for free or offer to address some of her

specific organizing concerns during the class.) Your class could last an hour, or two or three. It's great exposure to a number of people in your target market. They get to meet you, see how you work, learn some valuable organizing skills and tips, and have a fun time!

SELL A "DO-IT-YOURSELF" PACKAGE

If you're a "hands-on organizing only" professional organizer, for example, consider creating a new service that consists of an in-depth needs assessment and a detailed action plan. That way, the client can work on the organizing project herself, on her own time, paying a flat-rate price that's more affordable than hands-on services. (But be sure to price it high enough to cover your drive time, the actual needs assessment, and the time to create the action plan and any phone follow-up.)

CONSIDER "VIRTUAL" PHONE OR EMAIL CONSULTING

You may be able to offer this at a lower hourly or package rate than hands-on organizing because there's no drive time involved. Be sure to define upfront how many hours are involved, when you'll be available for calls, and how payment will be handled.

WRITE A BOOK OR EBOOK

It's nice to have a truly inexpensive option to give potential clients. Instead of closing the door on a hands-on organizing sale, open a window and make a book sale. It's still income, and perhaps customers will be so impressed that they'll call you back when they have the money to afford your services. This is an especially great idea if you have a choice client or niche. There are a million books on general organizing, but if you can share specialized tips (such as how to help senior citizens organize their paperwork, or how to stage a home for sale,) you'll have an easy audience! You can sell actual printed books or booklets, or offer downloadable ebooks.

CREATE AN AUDIO CD OR DVD

If you have a pleasant voice, why not put it to use creating and selling an audio CD? Pick a topic and share your organizing process and favorite tips. If you're comfortable in front of a video camera, go one step further and produce a video, so you can actually show customers how to get organized. (Just remember that neatness counts. Invest in quality when you produce your products.)

OFFER WORKSHOPS OR TELECLASSES

People will be able to gain organizing skills in a group setting at an affordable cost. It's also a great way to increase awareness of your services and build your database of potential clients. (And this is a perfect time to sell your books, audio CDs, and DVDs.) Or offer organizing teleclasses. You can set up a free conference call "bridge line" at www.freeconference.com. What a great way to highlight your expertise!

SELL SOMEONE ELSE'S PRODUCTS AT WORKSHOPS OR ON YOUR WEBSITE

If you find organizing products that you love, buy them in bulk and resell them at a higher price. If you have a website, many organizing product companies offer affiliate programs, in which you sell their products on your site (or direct customers to their sites with a link) in return for a commission on sales. For example, on your own website or blog, you might include affiliate links to a company that sells products you recommend. When someone clicks on the link, it is tracked so that any sales that result from it garner you a commission. It's great to make money with no effort! Amazon.com is another great avenue to earn affiliate commissions via your website. There are many great organizing books and products that you could highlight on your website or blog, and when your readers click through to Amazon and make a purchase, you'll receive credit for that sale. Learn more at www.affiliate-program.amazon.com.

choosing a business entity

There are four main types of business formations, described below. Most professional organizers are sole proprietorships, the easiest entity to form. Also increasingly popular is the LLC (Limited Liability Corporation). Generally, corporations work best for businesses with income of at least $75,000 per year, although it also offers the best liability coverage, so that is a consideration as well, even if you're making less than that. Please consider consulting an attorney or tax accountant to guide you through this decision.

SOLE PROPRIETORSHIP
It's the most common form of small business entities, with the simplest tax filing. Written documentation is generally not required to establish the business unless you're doing business under an assumed name. There are no limitations of liability.

PARTNERSHIP
It's similar to a sole proprietorship, except that two people are legally responsible. It has a simple business entity and tax filing, with written documentation generally not required to establish the business. (However, you should have a written agreement between partners.) There are no limitations of liability.

LLC
It combines the personal liability protection of a corporation with the tax simplicity of a sole proprietorship or partnership. But it may not offer the same tax savings as an S-corp.

CORPORATION/C-CORPORATION
Its owners are not personally liable for the debts and liabilities of the corporation so there is a separation of personal assets from business assets. It could have significant tax savings for higher income levels. You must hold regular meetings and keep written corporate minutes, and it has more complicated tax filing and consequences.

S-CORP
It offers liability protection of a corporation with simpler taxes and could have significant tax savings for higher income levels. You must hold regular meetings and keep written corporate minutes.

LICENSING AND EXCISE TAX
A word about licenses: Every city/county/state/country is different. Some require a business license and some don't. Some cities have zoning regulations and/or require a permit to operate a business out of your home. Call your local city or county offices to see what is required in your area.

TIP: Most states in the U.S. have a sales or excise tax for products and/or services. Some states require tax collection only on products sold within their state, while other states require it on all business transactions. Visit your Secretary of State's office or search online for its website to get details, or contact your accountant.

choosing a company name

In 2000, there were only about 1,300 NAPO members. Now there are approximately 3,500! While this growth is great for us professional organizers in most ways, it does present some troubles when looking for a unique company name. Newbies often complain, "There are no good names left!" But not to worry. Get creative. The perfect company name is just waiting for you to discover it.

Your company name has a big job to do. It has to help prospective clients find you, whether via phone directory, internet, or word of mouth. It should succinctly tell prospects what you do. It will create a first impression and the image for your company. And it must stand out in a sea of other professional organizing companies. That's a lot to ask from a little name, isn't it? Here's how to get the most out of yours.

MAKE IT EASY

Your company name should be easy to pronounce, easy to spell, and easy to remember. If it's hard to pronounce, prospects may move on to the next company name they see. If they can't spell it, they can't find you. And if it's not memorable, well, you get the picture.

CONSIDER HOW YOU'LL ADVERTISE

If your primary advertising source is a directory or roster that's listed alphabetically, you may want to consider a name that starts in the beginning of the alphabet so you get top placement. If your primary client source is your web page, alphabetical listing won't matter, but your company name should be easy to spell and relatively short.

FIND YOUR CHOICE CLIENT

Let your company name work for you by having it describe what you do, such as having the word "organizing" in your name. If you specialize, your name can help clients narrow down their search. For example, if you offer moving and downsizing services, a name like Easy Moves Organizing makes good sense. Prospects who need moving assistance are likely to contact you because your name instantly tells them that you offer the services they desire. Likewise, if you have a choice client, your company name can help him/her find you. For example, if you want to work solely with children, a name like The Organized Child will give you an edge over your competition. But don't let your name limit you. If you select Clutter-Free Closets, you're restricting yourself to closet organizing even if you decide down the road that you love to organize kitchens and home offices.

REMEMBER YOUR IMAGE

Your name is your image. It's your storefront. It's your first impression. Let it reflect your personality — are you fun and friendly or the down-to-business type? Just don't choose anything too weird or cute, or you'll regret it down the road. It's also fine to make your personal name your company name, such as Melissa Ashley Professional Organizing. Just remember that your name is now part of your image. Also, consider if the name will translate well into a logo of some sort. Picture it on your marketing materials. If the name is really long, it won't fit on a business card. If it's too ambiguous, it may be difficult to create a logo. Think beyond the sound of the name to the image it will create.

MAKE IT UNIQUE
Okay, so this can be tricky with thousands of other professional organizers out there. But it can be done! Start by brainstorming by yourself or with some friends. Write down every single word or phrase that pops into your head. Think nouns, verbs, adjectives, and adverbs. Then review the list, create word combinations, move them around, delete the bad ones, add some new ones, and narrow it down.

MAKE SURE IT'S AVAILABLE
Once you have a list of five to ten company name options, see if the names are available. If you are a NAPO member, you can do a company name search under the Member Directory to see if anyone else has your desired name(s).You should also do a web search for the names via Google or another search engine. Then, also search for nationally-registered names by visiting www.uspto.gov. Click on "trademarks," and then "search trademark database" and enter your proposed company name under "search term." If someone in another state has registered your desired name, it doesn't mean you can't use it as your company name in your state. But be aware you could be forced to give up your company name at a later date, so use caution when selecting a name that is already registered nationally. Some organizers offer services and products nationwide, so you may be creating confusion if you select a name already in use. Take the time to find the perfect name that will be unique to you and your business.

Once you've decided on your business entity type, you may need to register your company name with your local Secretary of State's office or County Register of Deeds Office. (This is especially true if you form a sole proprietorship.) Call the office prior to registration to see if your desired company name is available. A simple, one-page certificate of assumed name can be downloaded online, and you'll have to pay a small filing fee. Then, after the name is accepted, you may need to publish a legal notice in a newspaper in your county for two consecutive issues. For more information, see if your state offers a booklet called "A Guide to Starting a Business" or something to that effect.

if you don't want to be the boss

While most professional organizers own their own businesses, there are some who don't want the hassle of day-to-day business management. They just want to organize! If you're one of those people, you have a few options detailed below. You'll be glad to know that while most professional organizers are the sole organizer in their businesses, a growing number also supplement their organizing services with employees and/or subcontractors!

REFERRAL BASIS

You might work on a referral basis, taking jobs that other professional organizers pass on to you for a fee. Sometimes this is a one-time set fee, or it could be a percentage fee for all the income you make from that client for a certain time period. You won't have to sign a non-compete agreement. When you work on a referral basis, the client becomes your client, the check is made out to you, you accept 100% of the income, and the other organizer is not at all involved in the job once they pass the name on to you. You simply send the referring organizer a referral check per your agreement.

SUBCONTRACTOR/INDEPENDENT CONTRACTOR

You might become a subcontractor. In this scenario, another organizer is hiring you to do a job on an "as needed basis," giving you control of the project. But unlike referrals, you're working on behalf of the other company. (The client is not yours.) You may have to sign a non-compete agreement. You'll take some direction from the contractor, you'll need to report back to her about your progress, and she'll stay somewhat involved. You'll be paid according to your arrangement with the contracting organizer, not directly from the client. You'll be receiving only a portion of the fee charged to the client. For example, if the organizer charges $70 per hour, you might only receive $25-50 per hour when you get paid. In this scenario, you generally have your own organizing business and you will need your own business insurance. You'll be responsible for paying all of your own taxes and you won't receive employee benefits such as health insurance. You may (and should) work for multiple contractors and/or your own clients.

EMPLOYEE

If you become an employee of a professional organizing company, you may not have your own organizing business. You'll probably have to sign a non-compete agreement. You'll be on the payroll, receive a set number of hours per week/month, and possibly receive employee benefits such as insurance, a pension plan, vacation pay, or sick pay. You'll take direction from your employer — you won't be working independently — who has control over the working arrangement and will tell you what to do and when to do it. You'll probably receive training from your employer, and you'll use your employer's tools and equipment.

If any of these scenarios sounds interesting, you should start searching for established professional organizing companies that are looking for help. Most will want you to have experience, so practice! Start a portfolio of your work. Get client testimonials. Attend meetings of your local NAPO chapter, if there is one. Call other professional organizers in your area. Let them know you're looking for work. Be enthusiastic, confident, helpful, trustworthy and sincere. Show a willingness to learn on the job. Although there will be sections of this book that won't apply to you, please read everything. You'll need to know what your employer does on a day-to-day basis to better understand the complexities of running an organizing business.

working with clients

Working with clients is where you make your money, showcase your skills, and use your talents. In one word, it's awesome. This section will guide you step by step, from preparing your supplies to answering the phone, creating client contracts, doing assessments, staying safe, working with clients, and much more.

purchasing organizing products

Some organizers resell organizing products that they've purchased at local retailers or online. It's really up to you if you want to carry an inventory of products. Just note that if you resell for a higher price than you paid (giving you a profit), you'll have to get a state tax ID number and report the profit as income, filling out additional paperwork when you do your annual taxes. Clients may request that you shop for supplies for them, so make sure you determine if/how much you'll charge for your time. Some organizers charge full-rate for shopping (in other words, their standard hourly rate plus reimbursement for purchases). Others offer a discounted rate or do it for free for established clients. Some simply charge a mark-up fee, such as 25% of the original price of each product.

TIP: It's helpful to start creating a portfolio containing pictures of organizing products that you can show your clients when describing product recommendations or storage ideas that might be helpful to them. You could do this in a 3-ring binder, in some type of electronic document that you could view on your tablet, or via a Pinterest board. You'll also want to create a portfolio of photos of your past work. (Always ask clients' permission before taking photos. Some may feel embarrassed about their messes, so don't push it if you sense tension.) You should also start compiling a list of local resources, such as handymen, closet installers, housecleaners, junk haulers, psychologists or life coaches, as well as local donation sites.

preparing your take-along bag

What you bring with will depend on the type of organizing you do and each individual project. You can request that clients pick up some of the necessary supplies (such as file folders) before you begin, but never count on them to follow through with your supply requests. Remember, they are disorganized and will likely forget. Always bring along the necessary supplies. Pack up the basics in a professional-looking large attache, tote, or tool box. A gardening bag with side pockets also works well, as does a rolling cargo tool bag.

BASIC ORGANIZING SUPPLIES

- clipboard with fill-in assessment form
- breath mints, water, tissues, energy bar, band-aids, hand sanitizer, and cell phone
- receipt book or blank receipts
- extra business cards
- label maker plus extra cartridge tape and batteries
- pad of lined paper, pad of graph paper
- pens, pencils, felt-tip pens, Sharpies, and highlighters

- other little office necessities like a stapler, tape, paper clips, scissors, labels, calculator, sticky notes, etc.
- box cutter, letter opener
- tape measure and small tools (hammer, screw driver, level)
- assortment of nails and picture-hanging supplies
- furniture sliders
- cleaning rag or wipes
- gloves and dust mask (for very dirty or unsanitary circumstances)
- zip-top bags and garbage bags (heavy-duty, black)
- large cardboard or plastic boxes or baskets to assist with the sorting phase of your job

OFFICE OR PAPER ORGANIZING BASIC SUPPLIES
- all of the above basic organizing supplies
- one box each of colored and manila file folders, plus labels
- a box of hanging files
- a box of white labels for file folders

ADDITIONAL HELPFUL SUPPLIES
- clear, lidded boxes, such as Rubbermaid or Sterilite in shoe-box size and 15-quart size
- solid-colored cardboard photo boxes in neutral tones, like ivory, blue, or white
- magazine/literature boxes
- divided or modular drawer organizers
- 3M Command Hooks (including the large, metal variety)

CLOSET ORGANIZING SUPPLIES
- hanging canvas shelves, available in a variety of colors including neutral beige
- over-the-door pocket organizers in canvas or clear vinyl
- clear plastic drawers
- double-hang closet rods, available at home improvement and organizing stores

TIP: A special note about closet installations: You are not required or expected to install closet systems. But be able to recommend a good installer or two, as well as a quality do-it-yourself system. All building supply stores carry some nice basic systems. "Track and rail" systems (such as Rubbermaid FastTrack Garage Organizing System and elfa) are wonderful and sturdy. A main "hang rail" is mounted to the wall and all remaining pieces hang from this rail or track, so there's very little leveling and drilling involved.

your first contact with clients: the phone call

Most likely, your first interaction with a client will be by telephone or email. So having a scripted phone conversation or standard email reply to follow will be helpful. Many organizers create an "intake form" to guide them through a series of questions for the potential client. During this conversation:

- take good notes
- get to the root of their pain

- be likable and approachable
- it's important to remember to listen as well as talk

You'll use this time to decide if you and potential clients are a good match. This is often called "qualifying" clients. Do you offer the services they need? (Know your limits and your areas of expertise. You don't have to be all things to all people.) Do you want to drive to their location? Can you meet their timeline? Do you feel you're a good personality match with them? Do they make you at all uncomfortable? Do they have a realistic view of what a professional organizer can do? If you don't feel you're a good match, it's perfectly okay to recommend another organizer. A nice way to say this is, "I'd like to refer you to another qualified organizer as I don't think I have the skills to meet your needs." Or, "After discussing your needs, I think another organizer may be a better match for you." Then refer them to another organizer you know who better meets their need. If you don't know another suitable professional organizer, suggest they visit www.napo.net to find someone else.

The phone consult is also the time to clarify expectations: Share that you will be transferring organizing skills, rather than just cleaning up problem areas. Remind clients that disorganization is just a problem to be solved — not a character flaw — and you are their "coach."

Of course, you'll be asked for your rates. It's often the very first question out of prospective clients' mouths. Try not to answer it right away. The answer can scare off a client, who may immediately think, "I can't afford that!" Instead, simply guide the conversation the right way, understanding their needs, sharing compassion and understanding, and giving hope for an organized life. Once you tell them your fee structure toward the end of the conversation, they'll think, "How can I not hire this great person?" Another option is to soften the hourly rate with a package deal. You might say, "My hourly rate is $xx per hour, but many of my clients take advantage of my discounted package deals."

During your phone conversation or initial consultation, you may be asked for a time estimate for the project. Fight the urge to offer one. It's difficult to tell how much "stuff" a client really has until you get your hands into it. And remember the keep/toss/donate "decision-making" time varies by client. Some clients can make decisions quickly, while some agonize over each and every item. Things that carry emotional attachment can take a long time to sort through, as you listen to the stories that accompany the things. Some clients are easily distracted, and some have interruptions such as children or phone calls. There are just too many variables to allow you to give a realistic time estimate. If clients keep pushing for one, just tell them that you can try to give one after you have a couple sessions under your belt, but that the timeline really lies in their hands.

It's important that you talk about the experience they'll have during your organizing sessions and the results they'll see. If they can visualize their newly organized space and their more peaceful life, they'll be enthusiastic and motivated to work with you.

Nearing the end of the conversation, try to close the sale by telling them you're very interested in helping them with their organizing challenges and asking when they might like to schedule a session.

Once you book a session, it is helpful to mail or email clients a confirmation form/contract/ service agreement to detail the scheduled date(s) and time(s) of the session(s), your fee, and your cancellation policies. (See next section for details.) You might also give them a call a day before to confirm the appointment. Also tell them not to clean up before you arrive, since you'll want to see the space in its "natural" state.

If, at the end of the call, you don't seal the deal with a particular client, check back a week later. Don't feel you are being pushy. A brief call saying, "I just wanted to check back with you regarding your organizing project. It sounds like you could really use some help and new ideas, and I'd really like to be the one to offer them!" is enthusiastic and confident.

Be prepared for client phone calls, especially those first few. It all becomes very "real" in that moment, and you need to know what to say. Have your phone script or client phone intake form at your fingertips at all times. Know your rates. Be upbeat and positive. You can do this!

the client contract

You just booked an organizing session with a new client. Because your phone conversation was thorough, you understand her needs and feel comfortable that you can meet them. But did the client clearly comprehend *your* needs and expectations?

A simple — and necessary — way to define expectations is to send a contract before you meet. You can also call it a confirmation form, agreement, or policy statement, but whatever you name it, it meets the same need. It clarifies your policies so there are no misunderstandings regarding important details of your working relationship.

At the top of the contract, list the client's name, address, phone number, and email address. It's nice to have this info all in one spot (you'll bring a copy of the contract to your organizing sessions, in addition to mailing one out right away), and it gives the client the opportunity to notice any inaccuracies in the contact information.

Next, list the date(s) and time(s) of your scheduled session(s). This gives the disorganized client one more opportunity to enter the appointment on her calendar. (During your phone conversation, she may have jotted the date down on a scrap of paper and then lost it in one of the piles on her kitchen counter!) Then, list your payment expectations, such as when you expect payment (most likely at the end of the session) and the type of payment you accept (whether it's cash, check, and/or credit card). If you shop for organizing products for the client, list your shopping fee (if applicable) and how/when you expect payment for those items.

You might also define your trash and donation removal policies. If it's the client's responsibility, state it. If you assist with removal, list your fees, what you'll accept, and where you'll take it.

It's imperative to include your cancellation policy in the contract. Many organizers request 48- or 72-hours' notice for all cancellations. You'll need to decide what time frame works best for you. Determine what the penalty will be for no-shows, such as partial payment for the session (perhaps 50% of the session fee or a flat fee of $50 or $100), and if you'll offer a one-time "forgetful free pass."

The contract is also a great place to set personal expectations for the sessions and the relationship between you and the client. It's thoughtful and reassuring to include a confidentiality statement to let clients know that you respect their privacy. You'll be seeing paperwork and items that could be sensitive in nature, so assure them that you'll keep all client information strictly confidential. If you take before and after photos for your portfolio, let clients know they won't be used without permission. If you're a NAPO member, you may state that you adhere to the NAPO Code of Ethics. Perhaps you'll include your expectations of your clients as well. For example, you might ask that they be present without distraction (kids, phone, email, etc.) and communicate openly and honestly with you throughout the session.

If you offer a money-back guarantee on your services, state that in your contract. It's a great selling point and helps the client feel minimized "risk." You might also mention that all final decision-making is done by the client, so they feel more in control of the situation. You could also include a statement of insurance and/or bonding and any legal details recommended by your lawyer, if you have one.

Be sure to let new clients know that they'll be receiving your contract via mail (or email) before the first appointment, and ask them to sign it and scan/email or postal mail it back to you. Or, you could keep it simple and ask them to sign and return it to you at the first session. Simply sending the contract and knowing they read it is often good enough. (You could ask "Did you receive and review my contract?" when you call or email to confirm a day or two before the appointment.) Be sure to also include your contact information in case they need to reach you.

However complex or simple you make your contract, it's important that you feel comfortable with it and your policies. If you feel a need to have a lawyer review your contract form, by all means, do. Defining your business practices helps you set limits, feel secure, and look professional to clients.

TIP: A word about working with corporate or business clients. You may need to submit a proposal before you can be hired. It need not be complicated, but be sure to outline the reason they are contacting you, the goals for the organizing project, timeline estimate, fees, and payment schedule. It will probably need to be reviewed by some "higher-ups" in the company, such as bosses or human resources personnel before they can give you the okay.

---

assessments: connecting with clients

To be a successful professional organizer, you need to understand your clients' pain. It starts with a genuine concern for your clients, which leads to the desire to explore their needs, setbacks, limitations, motivators, and more.

The best time to learn about these things is during your initial client assessment. An assessment (sometimes called a "needs assessment") is a chance for you to visit the person's home or office and give it an unbiased look with fresh eyes. It's a time for you to ask lots of questions, do lots of listening, and then allow the client to hear your empathy and "big picture" plan for the project. It's an opportunity to break down the project into logical steps and roughly gauge how much time a project might take to complete.

CHARGING FOR ASSESSMENTS

The first thing you need to determine is if and how you'll charge for your assessments. Some professional organizers offer assessments for free, some for a flat fee, and some wrap the assessment into the first organizing session. Some charge but then credit the amount spent on the assessment if a client books a session. (Of course, some don't do them at all. But they're missing a great opportunity to truly understand the client and guarantee success.) The choice is yours. If you decide to charge for initial assessments, know that you're in good company. After all, your time is worth money.

Some pros to offering a free consultation:

- It gets your foot in the door and allows the client to meet and get comfortable with you.
- It may give you an advantage over POs who do not offer free consults.
- It allows you to see the situation to determine if you can handle the job.
- It allows the clients to get an idea of the strategy you'd use if they hired you.

Some drawbacks to offering a free consultation:

- You'll spend time driving there and back, plus the consulting time, and not get paid.
- You could possibly give away too much info and the client could try to do the job herself.

THE BENEFITS OF ASSESSMENTS

There are many benefits to offering an assessment. You'll get to meet the client to see if you "click." You'll be able to take a look at the home or office to see if you can handle the job and decide if you want to take the job. (For example, you may not know if a client is chronically disorganized (CD) until you visit with her in person. Perhaps you don't feel qualified to help CD clients, or you'd rather keep your number of CD clients to a minimum.) You'll be able to gauge the size and time commitment for the job better once you see the space. You'll get a feel for the organizing products and tools you'll need for the job. And, best of all, you'll give the client the opportunity to meet you, trust you, and, hopefully, hire you.

ASSESSMENT OPTIONS

Assessments can take many forms, from quick and simple to complex and time-consuming. A more complex assessment might involve a couple hours in the client's home or office, utilizing a multi-page assessment form, a detailed tour of the space, and lots of note-taking.

Following that, you would then spend a couple more hours in your office to create a personalized, written plan to present to the client. If you write a proposal/plan, be sure to spell out the desired end result, but don't give out the details of how to attain it. Unless you have a "do-it-herself client," you don't want to give away all your best organizing tips and techniques, leaving the client to think she can handle the project on her own!

If you have a client who wants to handle the organizing project herself and needs you to create a master plan to keep her on task, you will also write a detailed "how-to" plan. This scenario rarely happens, but once in a blue moon, you'll come across a client who has the willpower, skills, and determination to work alone — but with some guidance in the form of a written plan and possible occasional "check-ins" from you. This option can work well for someone who is on a tight budget but needs a little education and support from you. Take note to charge appropriately for the time you spend on the plan and client support.

A more simple assessment process might involve chatting with the client about his/her wishes and challenges, taking a quick tour of the space, and digging right into work. A basic assessment form is provided in Appendix C. You can also purchase a more comprehensive 5-page, fill-in-the-blank assessment form at the Time to Organize website.

Whatever assessment method you choose, make sure you bring the appropriate tools, such as a camera, tape measure, your portfolio, and, most importantly, your assessment form.

TIP: Just remember, this is a fact-finding mission, not give-away-all-you-great-tips time. You can give the client a run-down of the process (such as, "We'd start by tackling your desktop, purging your old filing cabinet, and creating a new, functional filing system.) But refrain from giving the specific "how-to's" of the job. (That's what they'll be hiring you to do.)

CREATING YOUR OWN ASSESSMENT FORM

Take the time to develop an assessment questionnaire that will help you get to the root of your clients' needs and pain. For example, you might ask questions like:

- Why do you want to get organized?
- How long have you been disorganized?
- Did you grow up in a disorganized household?
- Have you tried to get organized in the past?
- What are some of your biggest obstacles to getting organized?
- What areas do you want to get organized?
- How do other members of your family/staff feel about your efforts to get organized?
- Will other family members/staff members be involved in the organizing process?

- Do you have any tendencies toward ADD/ADHD, depression, or OCD?
- Do you have any special needs or medical challenges I should know about?
- What's your learning style? (such as visual, kinesthetic, auditory)
- How do you learn best? (such as reading, hands-on, listening, diagrams)
- Do you use a planner/calendar/smartphone to keep track of your time?
- How do you handle your to-do's?

- How do you handle time management? Do you use any kind of planner, calendar, notebook, smartphone, app, or computer program?

- What is working well in your home/office?
- What is not working well in your home/office?
- What items do you use/need most often?
- Do you prefer visible or hidden storage systems?

- How do you want to handle disposal of cast-offs (donation, etc.)?
- What time of day do you do your best work?
- How soon do you want to get started with an organizer (timeline)?
- Do you have a budget in mind?

Create a simple form to guide you through your first assessments, and modify it over time as you learn what you need to know from your clients. Remember, bigger is not always better. For a simple assessment, you might use Julie Morgenstern's four assessment questions found in her book, *Organizing from the Inside Out*: "What's working?"; "What's not?"; "What items are most essential to you?"; and "Why do you want to get organized?"

The following sections will go more in-depth on the questions you'll ask during your assessments. Remember, these questions are only suggestions. Use them as a starting point.

DISCOVER WHY CLIENTS WANT TO GET ORGANIZED

The first question to ask during an assessment is "Why do you want to get organized?" Maybe it's so they can find things when they need them, or to have more time for things they want to do. Perhaps they want to feel peaceful and at ease in their surroundings. Or they want to do better at work or get a promotion. Whatever their reasons, make sure they let you know so you can understand the motivating factors. This will help you seal the deal with prospective clients as you reiterate their needs and demonstrate how you can help get their lives on track, and, ultimately, assure success in helping them meet their goals. It may be helpful to know how long they've been disorganized (all their life vs. recently due to a difficult life event), if they've tried to get organized in the past (with or without a professional organizer), and what has kept them from attaining organization up until now.

DISCOVER WHAT CLIENTS WANT TO GET ORGANIZED

You may be called in to help organize one very defined space, such as a home office. Or, you may be contacted because an entire home or office just feels chaotic and unorganized. Sometimes, a client may initially think she wants to organize one specific space, such as the kitchen. But ask to see additional rooms (politely, and don't push if they say "no."). The entire home or office works together, so the organizational strategies you employ in the kitchen may affect the office; the living room may affect the kids' rooms; and so on. Ask for a list of all areas of concern, and start there. It's also helpful to know if family members (or, if in a business setting, officemates) want to be involved in the process.

UNDERSTANDING CLIENTS' ORGANIZATIONAL CHALLENGES

The assessment is an opportunity to learn why clients are disorganized. Perhaps they're making technical mistakes, like not defining "homes" for their belongings or owning more stuff than their space can hold. Or they have external issues, such as a highly demanding workload or uncooperative family members. Or frequently they have internal challenges, such as the need for abundance, unclear goals and priorities, or sentimental attachment and guilt. By asking the right questions (tactfully, please) and listening to the answers, you'll be able to provide answers, ideas, and hope for an organized life.

As you chat, you'll be able to determine if they are chronically disorganized (CD). During your assessment, try to work the following four questions into your assessments:

1. Do you have a diminished quality of life due to disorganization?
2. Have you been disorganized your entire adult life?
3. Have you made multiple, unsuccessful attempts to get organized?
4. Do you have an expectation of future disorganization?

If they answer "yes" to all four questions, then they are chronically disorganized. To better understand your CD clients, it's necessary to educate yourself. You will benefit from reading the book *Conquering Chronic Disorganization*, as well as visiting the website of the Institute for Challenging Disorganization (www.challengingdisorganization.org). ICD offers helpful teleclasses. Professional organizers who have been in business for a minimum of at least one year or are currently members of certain organizing associations are eligible to join ICD. If you plan to work with the chronically disorganized, it might benefit you to join at some point. NAPO also offers an excellent webinar on Chronic Disorganization. If you don't feel comfortable working with CD clients, it's okay to refer them to someone else, but it's advisable to get a basic education on CD so you know the right way to deal with such clients.

To successfully help clients reach their organizing goals, you'll need to ask many questions. Many revolve around their current organizational habits. Are they good time managers? What type of time management tools have they tried? Do they set aside time on a regular basis to maintain organization? Are they technologically savvy or do they prefer pen and paper? Are they creative (right-brained) or more logical and sequential (left-brained)? You might also get a feel for how they learn best. Are they visual, auditory, or kinesthetic learners? (More about this in the "In-Person Organizing Session" section.) They may not be able to tell you how they learn best, but you may pick up clues as you talk.

It's also helpful to know if your clients have any emotional or physical challenges, such as ADD/ADHD, OCD, depression, a chronic pain disease such as MS, lupus, or fibromyalgia, or limited mobility.

ASSESSING THE SPACE

Now it's time to get down to brass tacks — assessing the physical spaces to be organized. Take a tour of the room(s) to be organized or the entire home. Take notes while you walk and talk. Ask "What is working well in this space?" and "What is not working well?" Take measurements if helpful. Ask questions about how things come and go in the space. For example, if papers are piling up in the kitchen, you'll want to know what types of papers enter daily, who brings them in, and where they usually end up. You'll see patterns and habits develop. You'll also get a feel for the categories of "stuff" they own. What do they need daily vs. weekly vs. monthly vs. almost never?

What type of organizing products or tools do you see? Are they being used effectively? Do they need more/different organizing products? Is their space used wisely or would the room

(s) benefit from some space planning? Is the space big enough for the activities they want to do? What is the decorating style of the home? (modern, country, contemporary, urban, etc.). Do they prefer visible or hidden storage?

TIP: The space assessment is a very important step, but don't feel overwhelmed. With each one you do, you'll feel more comfortable with your assessment skills. Just don't let it drag out too long. Clients have a tendency to tell the room's "life story" at this time, so it's your job to move things along. Also, note any safety issues during this step. Do you smell any mold or mildew? Do you see any rodent droppings or menacing pets? Does anything make you feel unsafe? Take note. You need to decide if this client relationship will work, and you need to feel safe.

UNDERSTAND CLIENTS' EXPECTATIONS

The assessment is also a good time to clarify your clients' expectations of working with a professional organizer. You'll want to make sure they understand that they'll be working alongside you, learning organizing techniques so they can continue on even after you leave. You'll also want to make sure they can give you uninterrupted time — no kids, phone calls, or email checking while you're there! Do they seem committed to the process at this time? Likely, if they're calling you, they're now ready. But sometimes clients are just in the "thinking about it" stage.

Once you get a feel for the project, you'll be able to rough out a general outline for the project. Walk through this with the client, share some thoughts on how long the project(s) may take, and discuss pricing. (You may have already told the client your hourly rate on the phone, but now you'll have a better idea of the scope of the project. For example, is this a 3-hour job or a 30-hour job?) Will they need to purchase organizing supplies? If so, should they purchase them, and where should they shop? If you are shopping for them, detail your fees if applicable. If you think there will be a large amount of purging, consider costs for disposal. If you are not incorporating a "working session" into the assessment, then now is the time to agree on a date for their first session with you. It's also a good time to clarify your business procedures, such as payment requirements, fees, and cancellation policies.

ASSESSMENT CONCLUSION

Whatever you do, fight the urge to put the cart before the horse, digging in without knowing the cause of the disorganization. Of course, you're excited to start the hands-on organizing process, but when you know the cause of your client's disorganization, you can seek the remedy rather than just a bandage. Completing an assessment will show your client (or potential client) the value of working with you — a true professional! It's a great time to establish trust and weed out those people not ready to make the commitment to get organized. And it will also help you guide the project from start to completion so you meet your goals and find satisfaction and growth in every client interaction.

your professional image

Your attire will depend upon the type of organizing you're doing and where you're doing it. Your best bet is to match the level of dress that the client will be wearing, or go a step above that. Organizing corporate offices will require dressier clothing, such as a nice pants suit. Women, please note that skirts and dresses can get in the way if you're moving stuff around and digging under desks. If you're organizing in a home, khaki or dark dress pants work nicely. (But be sure to dress for your climate. Nice, dressy shorts are okay if it's hot and humid. For women, capri pants are a nice alternative to the "bare leg" look.) Bring an apron if you're concerned about dirtying your nice clothes. Generally speaking, no jeans unless you're digging in the dirtiest of basements or garages.

Wear comfortable, neat shoes. Many clients will expect you to take off your shoes in their homes. If you feel unsafe or uncomfortable in stocking feet, bring along a pair of slippers or clean, indoor-use-only shoes to switch into once inside. To show respect for your clients' homes, always take off your shoes or at least ask if they prefer shoes to be removed.

Also, be scent sensitive. Lots of people have allergies or simply don't want to breathe in lots of heavy fragrances. So skip the perfume and heavily-scented lotions and potions. And if you smoke, try to forgo lighting up before you meet with a client so your clothing and hair smell fresh.

A professional image should not be distracting. It will give you self-confidence and allow you to communicate with your clients, brand your company, and create an environment in which everyone is comfortable. It gives you instant respect and allows you to connect with the client.

the in-person organizing session

A typical consultation (organizing session) lasts 2-4 hours. Three hours is ideal for most people. Anything less than two hours and your client may not see a difference in the space and it won't be worth your drive time. Any amount more than four hours tends to exhaust clients, and you'll see them fade away. Of course, unique circumstances, such as a client who lives very far away from you or a client who needs to finish an organizing project quickly, may require a longer session. Those with ADD/ADHD or other physical or mental conditions may need to meet for shorter sessions.

FIRST THINGS FIRST: COMFORT, CONTROL, CONFIDENTIALITY

At your first session, you'll want to make clients feel as comfortable as possible. Remember, they may be embarrassed about their mess and state of disorganization. They may be nervous because they have no idea what you're going to "make" them do. They may think their homes or offices are the worst you've ever seen. They may come out and tell you this, or you may be able to read their body language. Either way, allay their fears by letting them know that your services are confidential. Whatever you see and hear is between you and them. And let them know that you are not going to make them throw anything away, nor will you discard anything yourself. Let them know that while you may encourage them to pare down in some areas, they are in the driver's seat at all times.

YOUR JOB: LISTEN, OBSERVE, TEACH, ENCOURAGE

Your sessions will be a mixture of active listening, teaching, and encouragement. The most important thing to remember is that all clients are unique, and it is your exciting job to get to know them and offer organizing solutions that fit their needs. You'll need to have an assortment of organizing ideas for a variety of organizing challenges because there is no "one size fits all" solution when it comes to organizing! This is where lots of reading, talking to other organizers, learning on the job, and even watching those addictive organizing shows on television come into play.

As you work with clients, you'll probably be asking lots of questions. For example, as you pick up an item, you'll often ask, "How do you use this?" or "When was the last time you used this?" And if you're reviewing their current organizing "systems," you might ask, "How does that work for you?" You'll be looking for habits, patterns, and dominant learning styles of your clients.

TIP: Throughout the session, be sure to watch for signs of fatigue or distraction in your client. Watch their body language to see if they are getting tired physically or emotionally. Remember, this may not be as fun for them as it is for you! (See the section "Client Clutter Causes" for thoughts on the why's and how's of client disorganization.) Suggest a quick break for a snack or beverage if needed. Help them minimize distractions by shutting the office door or suggesting they allow the voicemail to pick up messages.

Most importantly, watch for teachable moments during your sessions. Remember, in most cases, clients want to learn organizing techniques so they can stay organized for life. So as you're working together, tell them what you're doing at each step. Have them work alongside you, so you can see if they're understanding you. Don't panic at the thought of being a teacher. You don't have to teach them everything you know. Just the basics so they can process their "stuff" easily from here on out. Some of the simple organizing principles you might teach include:

- Keep similar items together.
- Assign a home for every object.
- Put away what you take out.
- Use containers to group similar objects.
- Label things so there's no confusion about where to put items.
- Daily, weekly, monthly, and annual maintenance are key.
- Abide by the in/out rule: when you buy something new, discard something old.

LEARNING STYLES

Visual learners process information through their eyes. They are the ones you'll encounter most often, as they make up 65% of the population. They tend to have lots of written communications, like to take notes, see pictures, and have reminders posted all over. You'll be using words like, "Let me show you," as you guide them through the organizing process. As you set up organizing systems, keep in mind that anything they can see will be helpful. Color-coding, charts, pictures, or anything they can keep visible may work well.

Auditory learners make up 30% of the population, and they process information through their ears. They respond well to the spoken word, so you'll need to give them good verbal directions as you proceed. It may be helpful to use voice memos, telephones, voicemail, tape recorders, and alarms to keep them organized.

Kinesthetic learners make up about 10% of the population. These people need to learn by doing. They can't sit still for long, love to move about, and use their hands for learning, exploring, and working. Rather than just telling them how to do something, they need to actually try out each process with you there beside them.

TIP: If you're not familiar with learning styles or need more information, do a little research at your local library as it will help you teach each client in the best possible way. Do an internet search for "learning styles" and you'll discover many helpful websites.

THE PROCESS OF WORKING WITH CLIENTS

You've probably read many "how-to organize" books. There are hundreds out there, each with unique techniques, products, and strategies. So how are you supposed to digest and learn all that stuff? Read as much as possible, but the way you'll hone your techniques is to practice, practice, practice! You'll discover what works best for many of your typical organizing scenarios. And, luckily, the six-step process outlined below will work with most organizing projects. You'll also see the following six steps "in action" when used in a kitchen organization project example, followed by a paper organizing project example.

1. Assess & Plan
2. Empty, Quick-Toss & Sort
3. Declutter
4. Declare a Home
5. Contain & Label
6. Clean Up & Maintain

---

1. ASSESS & PLAN

This step is only necessary if you didn't do an assessment at an earlier date or time. If you've chosen to forgo a comprehensive assessment, use a mini version. Now is the time to discover:

- why your clients want to get organized — what are the ultimate goals?
- what spaces to organize, what they look like, and what they need
- the clients' organizational challenges

Use the basic questions of "What's working well in this space?", "What's not working well in this space?", and "What things do you use most often?" Explore as you go and get more information as necessary.

Now, it's time to prioritize. What should you start with? As the professional organizer, clients are looking to you for complete guidance. Generally speaking, begin in the areas that are bothering them the most. But remember that all parts work as a whole. For example, if the pantry is driving a client nuts, that is the starting point for the day. But remember that the pantry works in conjunction with any other food storage areas in the home. Consider how much you think you can accomplish today and what you will do on subsequent visits. Run it past the client and see if the schedule is satisfactory.

Example: Kitchen - Assess & Plan Phase
Begin by analyzing your client's old storage systems. Were some things working well? If so, don't change them! If he insists on keeping his thermos on the counter by the coffee maker, stick with it. If it's convenient to have his recipe books on the countertop, keep it up. Now ponder anything inconvenient. How could you make those things work a little better? For example, if he hates having piles of cans and bottles littering his countertop as they await a trip outside for recycling, then make a new plan. For instance, clear space under the sink to install a pull-out trash can to capture those recyclables immediately after use. If he can't find his morning cereal because it's stuffed in the overflowing pantry, then that needs to be cleared out and reorganized.

Now, prioritize. If finding his food is the client's first concern, then the pantry needs to be reorganized today. Tell the client that you'll be emptying out its contents, as well as consolidating all food items from other locations, onto the kitchen island, table, and/or floor. If you'll be reorganizing all the dishware, utensils, and storage containers as well, discuss that. If you think you can get it all done today, tell him. If you think you'll need two or more sessions, let him know that now.

---

2. EMPTY, QUICK-TOSS & SORT
To begin any organizing project, designate a sorting area — clear some floor space or use a table, bed, or counter in the room. Then, item by item, remove each thing from its current spot and start sorting into logical categories. Each household is unique, so the categories will mirror the homeowner's lifestyles and priorities. What's important to them? What do they love to do? Create categories based on how they live (or want to live). Next, if there is a large volume of items, go a step further and create sub-categories. One great thing about sorting is that you'll easily see duplicate items, which will aid in the next step of decluttering. Some clients are great sorters and will jump right in. Others will struggle and need more direction in this area. Remember, you are teaching at all times, and so they are learning by observation. Don't just do it for them. Work alongside your clients.

Additionally, in many organizing projects, it's helpful to add a "quick-toss" to this phase, immediately tossing out items that are easily released before the sorting phase. If you see something obviously broken, stained, rusted, mildewed, unusable, or past its prime, now is the time to place it in the trash or, whenever possible, the recycling bin.

Example: Kitchen - Empty, Quick-Toss & Sort Phase
Take everything out of the pantry or cupboards. Check the quick-toss list to see what can be placed immediately into the trash. As you go, separate items into categories like canned goods, pasta, rice, baking supplies, oils and vinegars, spices, breakfast foods, snacks, etc. You'll see categories develop. Sort into subcategories if applicable. (Canned goods could be broken down into vegetables, fruits, tomato products, soups, etc.) Or, if working on the dishware, utensils, and containers first, take those out and start sorting into categories like everyday dishes, special occasion dishes, baking dishes, cookie sheets, pots and pans, cutlery, storage containers, small appliances, etc.

3. DECLUTTER

Essentially, this is the purging or downsizing phase. In the last step, you sorted everything into categories. Now you'll start decluttering. It will be helpful to have a few large boxes labeled "donate," "fix," and "relocate," plus some large trash and recycling bags. This is the stage where clients especially need support from professional organizers. If part of their goal is to declutter and downsize, the sorting phase will have shown them duplicate items. During this stage, a professional organizer can help them make decisions about whether to keep or toss. Try saying, "When was the last time you used this?" or "Do you really need four of these? Which is your favorite?" Those with emotional attachment and hoarding issues will have a difficult time with this stage. If your clients are overly sentimental about their stuff, try minimizing their physical contact with it. Allow clients to make the decisions, but help them realize that if they don't let go of some things, they won't reach their goal of decluttering or downsizing. As always, have that final goal in mind.

Example: Kitchen - Declutter Phase

If there are foods that are still good, but the client doesn't want them, suggest donating them to a local food shelf. If there is an overabundance of anything, point that out to the client. Did you unearth three dozen mismatched mugs? Are there any that can be tossed or donated? Is there a wide variety of plates, cups, and bowls? Pull sets together and select the favorite one. Can the others be donated or given to someone else? Assess pots and pans. Most people use two or three stockpots and two or three pans the majority of the time. Since pots and pans are quite bulky, encourage the donation of any not frequently used.

---

4. DECLARE A HOME

When assigning "homes" for categories of items, think about where clients are most likely to use certain items and the frequency of use. Pull aside the things they use most often, and store them where they use them and in easy-to-access areas. Keeping similar things together will help your clients navigate the space more easily. Put infrequently used items way up high, down low, or in the back. Where do they usually leave specific things? That may be where the home needs to be, and by actually designating the spot as its home, it's more likely to work. "Declaring a Home" can mean deciding in which room a category of things should reside. It can also mean deciding which piece of furniture they go in or on (including the purchase of new storage items like shelving or cubbies, as necessary) or where the furniture should be placed (including some space planning and furniture rearrangement if necessary).

Example: Kitchen - Declare a Home Phase

As you look over your groupings of kitchen items, plan to store them where they are used. For example, everyday dishes might work great directly above the dishwasher or close to the table. Perhaps pots and pans and cookie sheets could go near the stove. The coffee machine that is fired up daily should be easily accessible on the counter near the mugs, coffee beans, and grinder. Keeping similar things together will help your client navigate the kitchen more easily. If something is used frequently, keep it close and convenient. Where we put our stuff is as important as what we own. If we can't find it when we need it, or it's inconvenient to reach, it's likely we won't use it!

---

5. CONTAIN & LABEL

By placing some similar items in containers within their homes, you'll make storage spaces look neat and retrieval easier. You won't be containerizing everything, of course. But there are some very helpful organizing products out there. You can bring along some basics yourself (see the "Purchasing Organizing Supplies" section), use containers that your clients already own, or give them a shopping list. (Remember to take into account your clients' budgets and decorating styles that you learned during your assessments.) Be sure to make neat, easy-to-read labels for all containers so things return to their homes after each use. A label maker is a great tool for this task. Hanging or clip-on tags are an option for baskets or bins that don't have a smooth surface conducive to label-maker tape.

Sometimes it seems that you would containerize first and then assign a home. But in most cases, you need to first know where things will "live" before you can buy the correctly sized organizing containers.

Example: Kitchen - Contain & Label Phase

Now that you can clearly see categories and all the keepers, decide on the type and size of containers you'll need. There are many helpful organizing products available to keep kitchens orderly. Baskets and bins come in a variety of sizes and hold foods, like onions and potatoes, as well as cleaning supplies. A wall-mounted spice rack saves cupboard space. Inside cupboards, double-decker wire shelf-stackers double storage space. Wooden cookware racks keep pot lids tidy. An attractive vase or crock near the stove top corrals cooking utensils. A hanging over-door shoe bag on the back of the pantry door will neatly hold spice packets, Jello boxes, or kitchen gadgets. Label as much as possible so that it's easy to find what is needed. When putting away groceries or unloading the dishwasher, labels allow all family members to know the correct homes. To label a drawer, don't stick labels on the face of a drawer because it destroys the aesthetic appeal. Instead, put the label on the inside lip of the drawer so it is visible only when the drawer is opened. Likewise, inside a cupboard, label the front side of all shelves. Use a label maker to mark jars and canisters.

---

6. CLEAN UP & MAINTAIN

You've sorted, decluttered, containerized, labeled, and found the perfect place for everything. Now comes the most important part: teaching maintenance habits. If you skip this step, the space will quickly go back to being disorganized. How should your clients keep this space neat and organized? Perhaps they could take ten minutes each evening to return things to their proper homes. Maybe the "in/out" rule (see example below) would be good to keep the piles of clutter from returning. If other people live in the household, they should learn the new set-up and be told how to maintain it as well. Do your clients clearly understand the new organization system? Perhaps you'll leave them with an index card that lists daily, weekly, and yearly maintenance and tune-up information. Discuss a follow-up schedule so you can check back after a week, a month, and several months down the road to see if anything needs tweaking.

Example: Kitchen - Clean Up & Maintain Phase

Once the kitchen is organized, pat yourself on the back. Job well done! But you're not quite finished. Once everything is in its proper place, now is a good time to take the trash and recycling out of the house. Load donations into a vehicle so they are out of the way or call a local donation pick-up service. Grab the relocation box and help redistribute its contents to the appropriate rooms in the house, being careful not to get sidetracked into a new organizing project at that moment. (If you don't have the time or desire to help with the redistribution stage, it can be assigned as "homework" for the client to do later that day.)

This is also the time to discuss how this newly organized space will stay that way. Maintenance shouldn't take a lot of time, but it needs to be done with intention on a regular basis. Make sure you have created an "in/out" system where some purging takes place before the purchase of a new item. If a new set of plastic storage containers is purchased, an equal amount of old Tupperware should be donated. If a new mug comes home, an old one must go. It may be helpful to stash a donation box somewhere nearby as an easy reminder of this rule. Also, set aside time twice a year to check expiration dates on canned and boxed foods, as well as to do a quick-purge of old items in the fridge and freezer. Recommend setting aside time once each year to review the kitchen and all its contents.

You can follow this six-step organizing process for any type of organizing project, from closets to kids' rooms. But paper organizing does present some unique challenges, so here is an example of how to use the six-step process to get your clients' papers in order.

Example: Paper - Assess & Plan Phase
When working with clients to organize their papers, always start with an assessment. Some questions you might ask include:

- What types of papers do they receive on a regular basis?
- Where/how do the papers enter their home/office?
- What papers do they need to keep at their fingertips/easily accessible?
- What papers do they need to keep for archival or historical purposes?
- What do they need to do with the papers they receive? (act, file, delegate, toss, etc.)
- How do they handle their to-do's and do they keep/use a task list?
- What type of filing system are they currently using (if any)?
- Who else in the home/office needs access to the papers?
- How do they hope their lives will improve once their papers are under control?

The following basic system works well for most paper organizing projects. Of course, each household's needs are unique, and there are dozens (if not hundreds) of paper organizing techniques out there. Whether you use a simple file folder plus labels system or you opt to purchase an out-of-the-box paperwork organizing system (like Freedom Filer), you'll use the same process of sorting, decluttering, declaring a home, containing, and labeling.

Example: Paper - Empty, Quick-Toss & Sort Phase
Start on desktops, countertops, or urgently needed surfaces. The most recently received papers will be here, so round them up and place them all in a large box labeled "desktop papers."

Then, gather any papers that are on the floor or that are stuffed into paper bags, boxes in closets, or under desks and place them in a second box labeled "floor papers." (Resist the urge to start with these. They are likely older, less-needed papers.) It is important to round up all paperwork throughout the entire home if you are focusing on a home-based (rather than office) organizing job. Papers have a way of migrating throughout a home, and you'll need to see all categories of paperwork that are received on a regular basis.

Quick-toss things like junk mail, expired coupons, and manuals for items no longer owned. As a surface becomes clear, wipe down the shelves and/or sweep or vacuum the floor so it's a clean slate.

Once all the papers are rounded up, determine the types of papers received on a regular basis as you start sorting. Pick up the top piece of paper from the "desktop papers" box. Ask, "What is this? Do you need to keep it? Do you need to take action on this? Or do you just need to file it in case you need to retrieve it later?" Make piles, using large sticky notes to label the piles, or pop them into temporary file folders as you sort. You may end up using colored folders if that seems helpful. (Color jogs the memory for some, but not for others. For example, green might represent financial info or red for health papers.) Remember that we generally use only about 20 percent of what we have, so keep the goal in mind to toss as much as possible.

As you encounter papers that need to result in an action, put them in a folder labeled "to do" (such as a class to sign up for, an RSVP to send, etc.). Be sure to enter upcoming events immediately on calendars and then toss the paper invitation. As you encounter invoices/bills that need to be paid, put them into a folder labeled "to pay." As you encounter papers that need to be discussed with significant others or coworkers, put them into a folder labeled "to discuss." As you encounter papers that simply need to be read and then disposed of (magazine article clippings, newsletters, etc.), put them into a folder or basket labeled "to read." This is handy to take along when waiting in lines (such as at the doctor's office, dentist, bank, mechanic). Or the basket can be stored in the bathroom (really, a great place to read!), or near a favorite reading chair.

Example: Paper - Declutter Phase

At this point, the remainder of the papers should be either thrown out/recycled, shredded, or filed into "active" or "reference" categories. Remember, "active" papers are those that need to be accessed on a daily or weekly basis. "Reference" papers need to be kept but are rarely accessed.

Work through all remaining papers in the "desktop papers" box followed by those in the "floor papers" box, if applicable. You should find there is more in the "toss" category in the "floor papers" piles. Remember, only 20 percent of the things we file will ever be retrieved again. Another option for reference papers is to scan them and then toss them, creating a paperless filing system on the computer.

Example: Paper - Declare a Home Phase

Every household or office needs an appropriate type of file cabinet or box; the size will depend on the amount of papers one must keep. Once the papers are downsized and sorted, you'll have a good idea of the type and size of filing storage system needed. If a new file cabinet needs to be purchased, help the client estimate the amount of folders that need to placed inside, which will allow you to recommend the appropriate size of file cabinet(s) for the home or office.

Many households function well with a filing cabinet located in a home office or out-of-the-way space for papers that need to be kept only for reference. (Think tax returns or product manuals.) But there also needs to be a convenient place to store the "active," daily or weekly-used papers. For many, this is a filing drawer or a desktop file box kept in the home's hub of activity, such as the kitchen.

Example: Paper - Contain & Label Phase
Begin placing the file folders into a file cabinet, desktop sorter, or whatever combination of containers makes sense. Just don't cram too much into a cabinet or it will be difficult and frustrating to retrieve and refile.

Label folders and hanging-file tabs clearly, using a label maker or neat handwriting.

Straight-line filing (where the top file tabs are all on the left, middle, or right instead of alternating file tab positions) creates a clean line that's visually appealing and easy to scan.

Example: Paper - Clean Up & Maintain Phase
Take out the trash/recycling. Grab the relocation box and redistribute all of its contents appropriately.

Paper must be managed daily. Mail should be sorted as received, and junk mail should be tossed immediately. Everything else should be sorted into the active or reference-only filing systems. Homeowners should make time daily or weekly to file and can ask, "How am I going to use this?" Is it for a current project? File it in the appropriate folder in your active/desktop file box. Is it historical or for future reference? File it in the filing cabinet. Is it something that needs action, such as a class to research? Put it in the "to do" file. Is it something to be read? Put it in the "to read" folder or basket. Is it something that needs to be discussed with a spouse or coworker? Put it in the "to discuss" folder. Ideas to minimize paperwork include removing and replacing documents on an annual basis, such as insurance statements. Each time a file is opened to retrieve something, include a 30-second review to see what can be tossed.

Make a plan to maintain this space on a semi-annual basis.

client success

You've helped a client set up a fabulous filing system, complete with colored folders and neat labeled tabs. You sorted and purged and did everything a good organizer does. Job well done! But when you return a couple weeks later to help her tackle her next project, you notice stacks of paper throughout the house, the new filing system virtually untouched. What went wrong? Likely, it wasn't the structure itself, but the concept of maintenance that needs expanding.

Teaching clients to maintain their newly organized spaces is as important — if not more — than the system itself. Here are some tips to help clients have those "ah-ha" moments that allow them to keep the process going after you leave.

TEACH THEM NEW ORGANIZING HABITS
As you're organizing alongside your clients, tell them what you're doing and why you're doing it. They will learn by watching you (visually), hearing you (auditorially), and working with you (kinesthetically). Create quick and easy tips, such as "If you can do it in less than two minutes, do it now!" or "If you take it out, put it away when you're done." Help them adopt an in/out rule where some purging of older items takes place each time they bring home new ones. These things may seem common sense to us organizers, but they are new concepts to your clients. And never underestimate the power of visual clues, such as labeling all storage containers and areas.

HELP THEM SET UP SYSTEMS THAT MAKE SENSE
Nothing is worse than a complicated organizing system that falls apart after you leave. Get inside your clients' heads, talk them through their day, where stuff lands, and why it doesn't get put away. Work with your clients' strengths. Make things super easy to find and put away. Make systems fast, easy, and intuitive. Use creativity to create interesting systems and use innovative organizing products that keep them motivated. Make decluttering easy by placing a donation box in convenient locations. Help them get on mailing and calling lists from local charities that offer pick-up services, so regular collection dates are established. Give them checklists so they know what to do and can feel accomplishment as they check off tasks.

HELP THEM SET UP ORGANIZING ROUTINES
New habits take about 21 consecutive days to develop. So get clients off on the right foot by setting up schedules and routines to maintain their space. It's way too easy to let "organizing my papers" fall to the bottom of the to-do list, so instruct them to pencil in weekly maintenance times on the calendar. Use timers to help them realize that it really doesn't take long to stay organized, as long as they do it consistently. Even as few as 15 minutes a couple times a week might do it! And many clients need written instructions or reminders placed throughout the home, so help them create these before you go.

HELP THEM MAKE GOOD USE OF THEIR TIME
Clients often have so many to-dos that they simply freeze and do NONE of them! Help them learn to prioritize by discussing urgent/priority tasks vs. non-essential tasks, giving them permission to "delete" those that are no longer relevant or important to them. There are many systems to keep to-do lists: spiral notebook, smartphone, computer spreadsheets or notepad, folders, and tickler files are just a few. Even the ubiquitous sticky note can play a role. Use large post-its for priority-tasks, medium-sized ones for "do it soon" tasks, and tiny ones for "if I have time" tasks. You can place the post-its on a large poster board, grouping tasks by size. Or place them by size in three colored file folders (red for urgent). As they complete the tasks, they toss the stickies. Great for visual folks! You can also discuss delegation of tasks. We only have 24 hours in a day. If you think your client simply has too much to do and you've eliminated as much as possible, suggest delegating to a co-worker or family member. Or suggest hiring someone, such as a housecleaner or virtual assistant, if the budget allows.

HELP THEM GET PAST PERFECTIONISM

One of the reasons that some clients become disorganized is their tendency toward perfectionism. This, in turn, keeps them from making decisions, because they fear making the wrong decisions. Which means that nothing ever gets done. Teach them to shoot for "good enough." Help them see that by waiting too long, they miss out on great things. Have them ask themselves if spending more time on a task or decision is really in their best interest, or could they just be done now. Perfection stalls, but "pretty darn good" moves tasks forward.

HELP THEM SEE THE CLUTTER.

Professional organizers try to gauge the amount of client clutter during their initial phone assessments, but sometimes we're truly surprised when we get to their homes. They say they have just a "little clutter" or need just "a bit of help," but upon arrival at their homes, we can tell they lack "clutter awareness." Sometimes they simply don't realize how much stuff they truly have — it's built up slowly over time, so their sense of "stuff" has become warped. everything is important to them, without priority. To help them see stuff in its true light, try taking a paper towel tube (pretend you're a pirate looking through a telescope) and have them scan the room. This focus changes their perspective. You could also get a similar effect by taking digital photos of the room, zooming in on areas of clutter. Or you could show them how beautiful their space could be, if not for clutter. Bring a few issues of home magazines, and let them cut out pictures of rooms that appeal to them or have them peruse Pinterest for a few minutes. When clients can't "see" their own clutter, it's your job to gently bring it into focus.

HELP THEM SEE THAT THEY ARE NOT THEIR STUFF

You may have clients with an abundance of books. Helping them downsize their book collections can be a true challenge! Some type of super-attachment forms. For some, having lots of books around makes them feel smart and educated. This is an example of how clients can sometimes personify their stuff. Here's another example: A client has two sets of golf clubs. He hasn't played with them in the past ten years. But if he has the clubs, then by association, he is a golfer. Similarly, clients will often equate particular items with a person's love and adoration. They'll have a hard time letting go of clutter because "it was a gift from my niece" or "I inherited it from my great-aunt." Tell them that they are not throwing away the gift-giver's love. They are simply passing it along to someone who truly needs it, and they are making room for great things to enter their lives.

LEAVE EACH SESSION WITH A POINT OF BEAUTY

Your goal should be to always leave a space better looking than when you started. Even if you're in the middle of an organizing project, leave time to tidy up the piles. Leave counters and tables perfectly clear, except for an object of beauty. Place one of their favorite plants on the kitchen island, toss a lovely tablecloth on the dining room table, or artfully arrange just three items on their bedside table. These attractive visual clues will remind them to keep it neat from here on out!

FINALLY, BE THEIR CHEERLEADER

Yes, organizing can be boring to our clients. Make it fun by encouraging them to listen to their favorite music or make a beat-the-clock game out of it. Help them set up a reward system. For example, they might decide, "If I sort my mail every day for a week, I'll go out to lunch on Friday," or "If I sort through this pile of clothes and take the cast-offs to Goodwill today, I'll enjoy coffee with my best friend." Be their clutter-buddy or encourage them to enlist a friend for this role. And help them stay positive throughout the process. Place friendly reminders throughout their spaces, with positive images or quotations. Check in with them frequently by phone and email. Send them inspiring postcards. Finally, and most importantly, let them know they are not alone throughout their organizing journey! You are their rock.

disposal options

There are many disposal options. Ask your clients what they prefer to do with the items they've edited out. They'll look to you for recommendations, phone numbers, and details.

- **Donate:** Clients can give themselves a tax break and help others in need by donating items in good condition to a local charity. Some organizations, such as Vietnam Veterans of America, offer pick-up service. Do an internet search to find the options in your area.

- **Give to family/friends:** If clients find treasures that may be meaningful, they may choose to offer them to loved ones. But remind them that it's okay for people to decline their offers. Remember, we don't want to add clutter to others' lives!

- **Garage sale:** If clients have a lot of good-condition cast-offs (especially baby and kids' items, tools, or other highly desirable stuff), they might consider holding a garage/tag sale.

- **eBay:** Have a computer-savvy client? Try listing furniture, antiques, and other higher-value items online. Or take treasures to an antique dealer. Visit www.ebay.com for details.

- **FreeCycle/CraigsList:** With over 4,000 groups across the globe, the nonprofit Freecycle connects people who are giving and getting stuff for free in their own towns. Its mission is to reduce waste, save precious resources, and ease the burden on landfills. Visit www.freecycle.org for details. Craigslist (www.craigslist.org) is another no-cost listing service to try. It allows both giveaways and sale of items without any price bidding.

- **Trash:** Clients can rent a dumpster if they have a lot of unsalvageable junk. Or hire 1-800-GOT-JUNK, North America's largest junk removal service, to do it for them. They load the truck, and then recycle and dispose of their stuff as required. For smaller loads, consider the Bagster, which can be purchased at many local home improvement stores, loaded with up to 3300 pounds of waste, and then picked up at your convenience. Encourage recycling when possible; know the recycling guidelines in your area.

TIP: If your clients are considering holding a garage sale, remind them that sales are a lot of work, so this option is only good if they have time to dedicate to pricing, setting up, promoting, and staffing a sale. If they simply want to see their stuff go to a good home, encourage them to choose a charity that is close to their heart. As an added incentive, remind them of the tax benefits of charitable donations.

wrapping up

Watch the clock carefully. (But don't be obvious about it.) You'll need to allow plenty of time for clean-up at the end of each session. While the organizing job may not be complete, you want to leave the space looking neater than it was at the beginning of the session. Some organizers assist with the donation/waste removal process for their clients. Others do not. See the "Insurance" for more info about disposal cautions.

Before you leave, go over the plan to complete the job in upcoming sessions, if necessary. Some clients enjoy a little homework assignment to keep the job moving between sessions. Make sure that they know it is not mandatory. Ask them how they're feeling now. Relaxed? Tired? Motivated? Their words will give you clues to help them in future sessions.

payment

Because our clients are disorganized, it's important to collect payment right at the end of each session or have them pre-pay if you're offering a bulk discount. Make sure you write "payment expected at the time of service" in your contract/agreement so your clients know to have their checkbooks handy. If for some reason they "can't find their checkbook" at the end of a session, you might provide them with a self-addressed stamped envelope to make it easy for them to send you a check later that day. The exception to this might be if you're organizing for a business, in which payment is handled through the company's accounting department. You may need to provide these clients with an invoice and have them send you a check. "Net 30" (payment within 30 days) is typical for these situations.

Although most clients will be happy to pay by check, you might also consider accepting credit card payments. If you have a smartphone or iPad (with internet connection), you might look into the "Square," a small device that plugs into your smartphone so you can swipe and instantly process clients' credit cards. You pay a small fee per transaction and funds are sent to your checking account within 24 hours.

Pay Pal also offers a similar card reader with similar terms. Another option is to use Pay Pal to process your charges via your website for a nominal fee (about three percent of each sale).

Collect your payment and offer a receipt. Book your next session, if there is more to do, or thank them and promise to stay in touch for their future organizing needs.

follow-up

It's a nice touch to send clients a thank-you note right away. Then, a week after the session, give a quick phone call or email to see how they're doing. It lets them know you care and gives you a chance to set up a second session if you haven't already done that. A second follow-up call is important about two months after the session, and after that, stay in touch by email or postal mail on a quarterly basis.

You might also consider sending them an evaluation to fill out. This could give you a client's view of your work style, speed, communication, rates, process, and much more. Make it multiple choice or yes/no answers and they'll be more likely to complete it. Leave some room for client comments as well. Offer an incentive for filling it out, and enclose a prepaid envelope for easy mailing or use an online survey tool like www.surveymonkey.com.

when the client isn't there

Since skill-transferring is such an important part of organizing, it's imperative that the client is present for organizing sessions. (A whopping 92% of NAPO members stated that they work with the client present.)

However, occasionally, you may find a client who doesn't need to learn organizing skills. She simply doesn't have the time to get organized on her time. Or perhaps she's experienced an overwhelming life event, such as the death of a parent, the birth of a child, a divorce, a move, or an illness. In this case, she may pay you for your time and skill, not always your teaching ability. (Of course, these life events can also be a great time for learning organizing skills, but sometimes the job simply needs to get done ASAP.)

These jobs are a unique opportunity to organize in a new — and often fun — way. You'll first use your time to sort and categorize, make piles, and offer recommendations. (You should never throw anything away without a client's permission.) You can do the initial sort by yourself, but be sure to set up time at the end of each session to discuss your findings with the client, telling her what you've done and what decisions she now needs to make. She can then do the purge with or without you, and you'll return at a later date to do the placement and organizing of the remaining items.

It may be helpful in these situations to come up with some pre-determined criteria so you know what kinds of items you should place in toss/donate piles. For example, if you're organizing a closet, you might recommend that all clothing of a certain size be removed for donation and/or anything ripped or stained would be tossed. If you're clearing out a kitchen, you might set a rule that expired foods will be tossed. If you're sorting catalogs and magazines, perhaps you'd use the criteria that only the most current of each catalog and the prior 12 months' worth of each magazine would be kept and the rest recycled.

Remember, there is the potential for liability issues when the client is not present, so be insured, and trust your instincts.

client clutter causes

Why are some people more prone to clutter than others? Following are a few reasons. It may be helpful for clients to recognize what leads them to accumulate clutter in order to transition to a clutter-free life.

THEY INHERITED IT FROM THEIR PARENTS
Packrat parents often have packrat kids. And packrat kids can pass it along to their kids. The cycle continues.

THEY MIGHT NEED IT "SOMEDAY"
Clutter-keepers often insist something will come in handy "one day" causing overflowing homes and offices.

CLUTTER IS PART OF THEIR IDENTITY
Some clients use their possessions to create their identities.

THEY'RE BOMBARDED BY "MORE IS BETTER" REASONING
Catalogs and advertising invade your clients' lives and may add to the urge to buy more than they'll ever truly need. Or perhaps their "more is better" philosophy is due to their upbringing, low self-esteem, peers, etc.

CLUTTER FILLS A VOID IN THEIR LIVES
Clutter can help to hide loneliness, anger, fear, and other important emotions. When clients free the clutter, they'll free themselves to deal with the real issues around them.

Of course, you may not see your clients in any of the above scenarios. Perhaps they've simply accumulated a little clutter due to a shortage of time, too many work or family demands, or lack of organizing skills. This is perfectly normal. But for those who know that clutter is negatively affecting their lives, the above reasons may help define the source and allow them to start the decluttering process.

On the other end of the spectrum, some clients suffer from chronic disorganization (CD) and may need the help of an organizer who specializes in CD. Perhaps you'll need to refer this type of client to another organizer in your area. Or, if you'd like to learn more about CD, start by reading Judith Kolberg's book that is referenced in the "Educational Resources" section of this book or take the NAPO webinar on chronic disorganization.

tricky client scenarios

There is no better way to learn how to work with clients than to "just do it!" No book could ever prepare you for all the situations and challenges that you'll encounter as a professional organizer. However, here are a few tricky scenarios and some insider's advice.

NO-SHOW STAN
You arrive at his house on time, ring the bell, and no one answers. Stan forgot all about your appointment! **Insider's Tip:** Be sure to call him the day before to remind him of the appointment. This is not an opportunity for him to back out of the appointment; rather, it's a courtesy call to let him know you're looking forward to working with him tomorrow.

BUSY-MOM MEGAN
After you step into her house, you realize her three young children are home. They demand mom's attention, and mom is not able to give you, or the organizing project, hers. **Insider's Tip:** Let her know ahead of time that she should make arrangements for a babysitter if she has kids. You know how valuable her time is, and you want her to be able to work without distractions and get her money's worth out of your time together.

DISTRACTED DON
You're working with Don in his busy office, helping him set up a new paper management system. However, people keep popping in the door, the phone keeps ringing (and he keeps answering it), and he just can't stay focused on your task. **Insider's Tip:** During your initial assessment or phone consultation, let him know you'll need his undivided attention during your organizing session. He'll need to tell his staff that he's unavailable during this time, shut the door, turn down the phone ringer, shut off the cell phone, and close down the email.

NEARLY-PERFECT PAULA
You arrive at her house and are startled to see the home in immaculate condition. What could you possibly organize for her? **Insider's Tip:** Before you panic, realize that if she called you, there must be some area that is bothering her. Sometimes, homes look organized and neat on the surface, but when you open the closets and cupboards, you see chaos. Or, maybe she's just looking for new storage ideas or products. Be sure to clarify her expectations during the phone consultation so you know how to best help her. If she wants product recommendations, make sure to bring photos and catalogs of organizing products. If she's just feeling stressed out because she's not managing her time well, you'll work on new strategies to get life under control. You are there to help however you can, no matter how big — or small — the physical mess.

CAN'T-LET-GO GAIL
She admits that she's a bit of a packrat, and at your first meeting you realize that she's not ready to let anything go. It's frustrating because it's hard to organize a home that has twice as much stuff as it needs. **Insider's Tip:** It's always good to ask upfront if a client thinks she has too much stuff. Very often the answer is "yes." Follow by asking if she's ready to part with some of it to make room for the things in her life that she truly loves. Let her know you'll guide her through that process gently. Offer a variety of disposal choices, including selling/consigning, recycling, donation, and disposal. Be well-versed on all options, including knowing the names and phone numbers of local stores and charities. If her answer is

"No, I'm not ready to let go of anything," then perhaps she is not yet ready for a professional organizer, or perhaps she's chronically disorganized and could use the assistance of an organizer who specializes in Chronic Disorganization.

CHRONICALLY-DISORGANIZED DANIEL
You've had a couple sessions with him, but each time you come back, it looks worse than last time. You wonder what's going wrong. Is it your fault? Why can't he keep up the systems you've developed? **Insider's Tip:** First off, talk to him about how the systems are working from his point of view. Perhaps they are too complicated or just not meshing with his lifestyle. Offer to tweak the systems a bit. If that still doesn't work, you may discover that he is "chronically disorganized"(CD). (Read *Conquering Chronic Disorganization* for great information and organizing techniques to help clients like this.) If he's been disorganized most of his adult life, he's tried unsuccessfully to get organized in the past, and his disorganization is negatively affecting the quality of his life, he is chronically disorganized. It is perfectly acceptable to refer him to another organizer who specializes in CD if you feel underqualified. If you continue on with him as a client, recognize small successes, realize that he may need regular "maintenance" visits, and educate yourself on new techniques that work especially well for people with CD.

UNACCOUNTABLE URSULA
You know she isn't chronically disorganized, but she's not making any headway between organizing sessions. Her paperwork is out of control! Why isn't she taking the time to handle the mail as it arrives, pay her bills on time, and keep her counters clear of clutter? **Insider's Tip:** Perhaps she's simply not scheduling the time to maintain the systems you've set up. Sit down with the client and her calendar, and schedule regular times to handle paperwork. Perhaps each Tuesday and Thursday morning from 9:00 - 10:00 or Sunday evenings from 8:00 - 10:00. Have her select a time that works with her internal clock. Once it's written on the calendar — like a real appointment — she'll probably remember to do it, and it will become a habit. Remember, your goal is to have your clients maintain an organized home, office, or schedule even when you're not there. Perhaps you'll even want to give her a phone call before or after her "paperwork management" times, just to check in.

RELUCTANT RON
His wife called you, requesting an organizing session to "clean up his mess." Alarm bells sound in your head, but you go anyway. Upon arrival, Ron is uncooperative and you leave feeling frustrated. **Insider's Tip:** Listen to those alarm bells in your head! Anytime someone calls on behalf of another person, you should ask some careful questions: "Does the disorganized person know you're calling a professional organizer?" "Has he expressed a desire to get organized?" "Could I speak directly to that person?" Never show up for an organizing session without first speaking to the disorganized potential client. Perhaps if you had simply spoken to Ron on the phone, listened to his story, and offered empathy and solutions, he would have jumped on board. Or maybe not. But either way, you wouldn't be stuck with someone who doesn't want you there.

SHOPAHOLIC SHERRY
Your new client, Sherry, has shopping bags all over her house. She has clothes in her closet with tags still on them. Her days consist of thumbing through catalogs and running errands (which result in more "stuff" entering her home). She needs more than an organizer... she needs to quit shopping! **Insider's Tip:** Shopping is a part of our culture. But sometimes, it turns

into addiction. It becomes a compulsive disorder which brings a temporary high. This excessive, chronic, and impulsive behavior can destroy a person's finances and relationships. (It goes way beyond a weak-moment shopping spree.) Help may come in the form of Debtors Anonymous meetings, credit or debt counseling, and professional assistance from a therapist. If you suspect this addiction, it may be difficult to bring up. But you can't help her if there are major underlying issues. Tactfully have a conversation about why she shops so much, and if she seems open to the idea, offer a referral to a therapist.

These are just a few of the scenarios you may encounter as a professional organizer. Of course, most clients will be delightful to work with, appreciative of your skills, and open to your suggestions. But awareness is key to ensuring that when difficult situations arise, you can handle them like a pro!

hoarding and shopping addictions

In addition to chronic shopaholic clients, there are those who save. Some people "save things," and some people save everything. When it gets to the point that a home is nearly uninhabitable, compulsive hoarding may be the culprit. People who suffer from this psychological condition see the value in every object, leading to the inability to get rid of things (even items of no value, such as old newspapers and food containers).

Hoarding is more extreme than simply accumulating clutter. Hoarders may not be able to move around the home. Floor space may shrink to a single pathway. Hoarding restricts everyday activities like cooking, cleaning, or sleeping and severely reduces the quality of life. Hoarders may not even recognize the extremity of their surroundings. Or, if they do, they may refuse to let family and friends visit their homes for fear of being criticized.

If your client has symptoms of hoarding or shopping addiction, consider referring her to an experienced professional organizer. As a newbie, your well-meaning efforts could backfire. It's best to leave this type of client to an expert veteran organizer. Also, encourage the client to contact a therapist so she can form a support "team." Good resources for basic information are the Institute for Challenging Disorganization and the International OCD Foundation (IOCDF) at www.challengingdisorganization.org and www.iocdf.org.

physical safety tips for professional organizers

Although you will likely feel quite safe entering complete strangers' home on a regular basis, always trust your instincts. Following are some personal safety rules you might enact. You may want to come up with a few of your own and write them down.

- Use your initial phone conversation with a new client to probe around a bit. Do they live alone? Do they prefer to meet during daytime hours or evening/weekend hours? Take note of the person's tone and mental status. If anything about this potential client makes you wary, it's best to pass on the job. Trust your instincts! If it doesn't feel "right," it isn't.

- Use the internet to your advantage. Google your potential client's name and state. Poke around on Facebook. You never know what will show up.

- You might consider meeting some clients beforehand at a coffee shop to get to know them. That way, if you get that creepy feeling as you sip coffee, you can simply tell them that you're not a good fit or you don't have the skills necessary for the job, and you can walk away gracefully (and safely).

- Female professional organizers especially need to set their own safety standards. You'll need to decide if you will allow yourself to be in a home or office alone with a male. Some organizers decide that they will decline male residential clients unless a spouse/significant other of the client will be home.

- Realize there is no "safe" category of clients. Female clients can be as emotionally unstable as male clients. Don't discount half of the population based on gender. Just be aware of your comfort zone.

- If your client tells you s/he has a physical or mental condition, it will be helpful for you to research it a bit before your session. Be especially careful when working with a person whose symptoms could include mood swings, irritability, or depression. It is not uncommon to work with clients who have ADD/ADHD, OCD, depression, or other mental health issues.

- Keep your personal information private. Use a separate phone line for your business (cell phones work great) and a post office box instead of your home address. Or simply don't list an address on your materials at all.

- Always make sure a family member, coworker, or friend knows your whereabouts. Keep a copy of your schedule and clients' addresses in your office and make sure clients are aware that someone always knows where you are and when you'll be back.

- Carry a cell phone, and keep it in your pocket (not your bag) at all times. Have an emergency plan, including a friend to call for help and a "panic code" to use. Also, ahead of time, create a convincing, non-confrontational lie prepared to explain a hasty exit if you feel threatened. For example, "My child/friend/spouse is sick and I need to leave to pick them up right now." Or, "I forgot something in my car. I'll be back." If you need to leave your organizing materials there, so be it. You can always go back later to get them with an escort. If you feel uneasy, get out immediately!

- Always know where the closest exit is in relation to where you are in the client's space.

- Do not accept food or beverages from clients unless you know and trust them well.

- Most important: If someone triggers your "uh-oh" feeling, don't stop to analyze it — just get out! You'll have plenty of time to figure it out later.

providing stellar customer service

Whether you want to prompt return customers or solicit referrals from past ones, providing top-notch customer service is essential to stay ahead of your competition. Think about it... there are probably dozens, hundreds, or even thousands of other people who could offer what you do. But can they do it with thoughtfulness, mastery, and flair?

Here are some easy ideas you can try to wow your clients:

- **Be there when they call.** Answer your phone before the voicemail picks up, and make sure to be pleasant and attentive. If you can't be there to answer the phone, have a pleasant voicemail message that inspires them to actually leave a message rather than moving on to the next person on their vendor list. And return calls as soon as possible, preferably within a few hours and definitely within 24 hours.

- **Make a good first impression.** Arrive on time for all appointments, prepared and ready to serve. Have a neat appearance, appropriate attire for the setting, and a clean vehicle. Don't forget essential supplies.

- **Give your full attention during client visits.** When you're with clients, show respect and courtesy by not accepting calls on your cell phone or checking texts. Be empathetic and let them know they're your priority at that moment.

- **Be a wealth of information for your clients.** Anticipate their needs and be helpful even if it means going above and beyond your normal scope of duties. Be in-the-know about products and resources that might be beneficial to them. Be able to provide names and phone numbers of your recommended service professionals. And always give them more than they expected, such as a coupon for a future discount, a free product, or personalized resource lists.

- **Thank them.** At the end of appointments, thank clients for choosing you. Sounds simple enough, but it's easy to forget. And then send another thank-you in the form of a note or email the next day.

- **Send a small gift as a token of your appreciation.** Consider delivering a small bouquet of tulips or daffodils or a box of delicious chocolates after your first visit (or at the end of a big project), or send a gift card to a local coffee shop.

- **Follow up with a check-in phone call a week later.** Your clients will be impressed that you still care even after you have their money. And let them know you love referrals. If you don't ask, you won't receive.

- **Stay in touch.** Send a tip-filled e-newsletter in your area of expertise. Or, if you see an article in the paper that might be of interest to a client, clip it out and send it to him/her. The same goes for information about a new product or resource that might intrigue a client. Also, consider sending holiday or birthday cards to let clients know you care.

With these tips, you'll be able to make every client feel like your most important one. What a great way to distinguish yourself from your competition, make your industry look great, and add value to your service!

marketing your business

marketing myths

To most people, marketing is a mystery. It sure sounds sneaky, complicated, and expensive. But marketing doesn't have to be any of these things. Let's begin by setting the record straight on seven common marketing myths, so you can get on track and start promoting yourself with ease.

Myth #1: When marketing yourself, you must be all things to all people.
Reality: As you develop your marketing ideas, try to find one specific group of people to be your "target market." For example, is your choice client a stay-at-home mom, a time-starved business executive, or a downsizing senior? It might help to get a picture in your head of your choice client and even "name" that person. So every time you sit down to contemplate your marketing strategies, you'll picture "Stay-at-Home Stacey" or "Evan Executive" or "Downsizing Dottie." Then, as you develop your marketing plan, you can ask yourself how your target audience would best be reached. If your choice client is Stay-at-Home-Stacey, what publications would she read? Where would she hang out? What types of services or products does she need? What is her pain? How can you help her? If you can visualize and relate to her, you can better sell her your services and products.

Myth #2: Marketing must be expensive in order to work.
Reality: Many successful marketing strategies don't cost a thing. How about sending a press release to your local paper? (See the "Free Media Coverage in Newspapers" section of this book if you're unsure how to do this.) The public will get to know you through the eyes of the reporter, and they'll tend to trust the information presented much more than if you spent tons of money to deliver the same information via a paid advertisement. How about setting up a great incentive referral program for your current and past clients? There is nothing as great as positive word-of-mouth to generate new clients. Brainstorm ways to promote your business without breaking the bank.

Myth #3: It is scary and intimidating to deal with the media.
Reality: Reporters and editors are people just like you. They depend on the public to tell them what's new, what's important, and what's hot in our part of town. They appreciate a well-written pitch letter and a nice follow-up phone call. They also love it when you're quickly available to take their calls and when you make good use of their limited time. Never be afraid of the media, but always be prepared for their call. Remember, if you're not available or helpful, they'll move on to your competition for the same information and exposure.

Myth #4: You're on your own when it comes to marketing your business.
Reality: Developing alliances with other people will help you promote your business. Develop a cross-referral program with a complementary (but non-competitory) business, such as a housecleaner, real estate agent, feng shui expert, life coach, wardrobe consultant, or closet designer. Brainstorm ideas that will help you promote each other's businesses, share each other's databases (with client permission, of course), learn from each other's mistakes, and copy each other's marketing success strategies.

Myth #5: You must be a polished speaker, brilliant writer, and masterful graphic artist to market your business like a pro.
Reality: Not everyone is good at all (or any) of these things. Capitalize on your strengths, and use them to promote yourself in a way that feels natural to you. Does public speaking make you weak in the knees? Capitalize on your other strengths, such as your writing aptitude or great one-on-one conversations. Does your writing leave something to be desired? Then use your other talents, like your great rapport with people or your brilliant photography skills, to market yourself. Do what you do best, and hire out the rest. Don't be afraid to spend some money to hire pros to make you look good.

TIP: If you want to outsource some of your business tasks, consider a service trade to save money. Offer your services to a local writer, designer, or artist and swap your talents so you can both benefit. You could swap hour for hour or dollar for dollar, or work on a project basis.

Myth #6: Marketing must be under-handed and sneaky.
Reality: Marketing can be educational and a great way to showcase your expertise. Always be honest in your advertising claims, offer helpful information, make it clear how to contact you, and make good on your promises. And try to be authentic in whatever way you promote your business. People can spot "fake" a mile off!

Myth #7: If your marketing efforts don't yield immediate results, then they don't work.
Reality: Repetition is the key to visibility and success. An advertising rule of thumb says it takes at least five to seven points of contact before consumers associate your service or product with your advertising. That means that you'll need to offer your marketing message multiple times before potential clients will purchase from you. So send educational and interesting monthly or quarterly mailings. Keep up with those sales calls. Offer specials. Stay in the media spotlight. And keep networking. When your client is ready to buy, you want to be the one who gets the call. It will likely pay off eventually, even if it doesn't seem like it today.

Now that these marketing myths have been revealed, you'll read dozens of great marketing techniques. It's up to you to take the next step to decide which marketing ideas are right for you.

50 ideas to market your business

Need some marketing inspiration? Here are 50 ideas to get you going. Some cost a little money, some cost a lot, and many are free! Select the methods that intrigue you the most, and then add a few more as you learn what works best for your company.

ADVERTISING

- Create a first-class website.
- Make sure your website is well-optimized so it is top-ranked in the major search engines.
- Run online ads, such as Google AdWords or Facebook ads.

- Advertise in local print newspapers and magazines that directly reach your target audience.
- Get a listing in your local phone book only if your target audience regularly uses one.

PUBLICITY
- Seek PR in your local papers, perhaps revolving around a national organizing holiday, a seminar you're giving in your community, a contest you're holding, a product you've developed, or time you've donated to a local charity.
- Write articles for local and national papers.
- Submit articles to online publications that reach your target audience. Request that your name and web address be included at the end of the article.
- Book TV or radio appearances.
- Offer to speak to the local PTA or teachers.
- Offer to organize a radio station studio or reporter's desk in exchange for publicity.

NETWORKING
- Plan to attend your local NAPO chapter's monthly meetings, if available. They are usually open to the public. (Some charge a small guest fee.) You will meet professional organizers, as well as others like you who are considering a career as one. Visit www.napo.net to locate the chapter nearest you.
- Investigate trade and business associations, including local Chamber of Commerce and small business networking groups (such as National Association of Women Business Owners and Business Networking Int'l).
- Discover related and complementary fields, such as a housecleaning, real estate, feng shui, life coaching, wardrobe consulting, and closet designing.

TEACHING/SPEAKING
- Write your "30-second commercial" so you can easily and articulately explain what you do when you meet new people.
- Develop seminars/workshops for local businesses on time management or office organizing.
- Create workshops/classes for adult community ed on topics such as organizing for kids and homes, time management, clutter control, and simplifying life.
- Offer a free 30-minute teleclass or webinar on the organizing topic of your choice.
- Target mom's clubs and churches.
- Contact your local community college to speak to students or staff.

DIRECT MAIL
- Write and send newsletter/tips to past and potential clients.
- Send birthday cards to clients.
- Send "thinking of you" cards to clients to check in between appointments.
- Mail referral thank-you cards.
- Mail to local professionals in related fields: psychologists, Realtors, builders, etc.

SOCIAL MEDIA
- Set up a Facebook page, and create Twitter, Instagram, and LinkedIn accounts.
- Start a Pinterest page showcasing your favorite organizing supplies and products or photos of great organizing solutions and creative organizing ideas by room.

EVENTS

- Play off special events/organizing days.
- Participate in expos/trade shows.
- Sponsor a "Messiest Desk" or similar contest.
- Offer a special "limited time" deal.

REFERRALS

- Create an incentive program for current clients to encourage them to refer family and friends to you. Give them a few extra business cards to pass along to friends.
- Develop a cross-referral program with other professional organizers in your area.
- Consider charging a referral fee for leads sent to other organizers.

PARTNERING/ALLIANCES

- Find one or more complementary businesses to develop a cross-referral program, such as a housecleaner, Realtor, feng shui practitioner, life coach, wardrobe consultant, and/or closet designer.

APPRECIATION GOES A LONG WAY

- Send thank-you gifts.
- Send thank-you cards.
- Offer discounts to past clients.

UNIQUE WAYS TO MARKET

- Turn your car a moving billboard with magnetic signs or stenciled windows.
- Purchase or create magnetic business cards.
- Create a photo album of your "before and afters" to show what you do.
- Offer gift certificates or gift cards.
- Wear your name tag or clothing with your company logo when you're out in public — you never know who will inquire about your services.

PRINTED MATERIALS

- Always carry business cards — you never know who you'll meet.
- Post marketing brochures and/or business cards on public bulletin boards at local coffee shops, cafes, grocery stores, etc.

PRODUCTS

- Sell other vendors' products at a marked-up price as an additional stream of income.
- Sell others' products on your website through affiliate programs.
- Develop your own new products.
- Write tips booklets or a how-to book or ebook.

Now that you have 50 solid ideas to market your business, it's up to you to pick your favorites — based on your budget and personality — to try out. Put them down on paper and dedicate time each day or week to make them happen. Take note about what works best to make your business grow.

marketing best bets

There are nearly unlimited ways to market your business. It can be intimidating to decide which methods will yield the best "bang for your buck." The following five methods will likely provide you with the majority of your new clients. You need to decide what will work best based on your budget, clientele, resources, and personality. You'll find more detailed information about each one following this list.

- having a professional-quality website
- maximizing social media marketing
- writing press releases and getting free exposure in local publications
- asking for referrals from clients, friends, family, and colleagues
- seeking out speaking engagements with your ideal client base

creating a stellar website

You can get a simple website up and running at a variety of price points. Ask other small business owners in your area for a recommendation for a qualified and affordable web designer. This is one area where it's best not to skimp. Your website is your storefront, so make it the very best you can afford.

Creating a powerful and productive website starts with a little planning and goal setting. A truly stellar website is created with intention. Begin the process by writing down your goals. What do you want your website to do for you? You'll have both primary and secondary goals. Of course, you'll want the site to generate client leads. But you might also want it to establish your credibility in your field, provide helpful information and resources, and/or to answer questions about the organizing process. Come up with a list of at least two primary goals and four secondary goals.

Once you have your goals written down, you can rough out your website. Most professional organizers can get by with four to six pages. At the very least, you'll need a Home page, About Us, Services, and Contact Us. If your time and budget allow, you should consider some other pages that will help your clients understand more about you, such as Testimonials, Portfolio, FAQs, Resources, and Tips.

You might peruse other professional organizers' websites first, looking for ideas. This is fine! But when it comes time to start writing, you need to close down those inspiration websites. It is all too easy to start writing your rough draft, grabbing bits of text from this website and that, and suddenly, you've plagiarized (stolen!) text from a seasoned professional organizer. Even copying a single sentence is illegal, let alone an entire paragraph or page. While unintentional, you will be highly embarrassed when the colleague contacts you to discuss the issue. (And they will, thanks to copyright search websites like www.copyscape.com.) Trust in your writing skills and know that you can create your own unique words to tell your story.

The next step is to begin writing your website text. You can do this yourself if you enjoy writing and have a good mastery of grammar, punctuation, spelling, word flow, and compelling statements. (If you are not a stellar writer, it may be a good idea to hire a copywriter.) As you create your web copy, always keep your target market in mind. What would make them want to work with you? What do they need most? Why are they visiting your site? What kind of information can you provide that is interesting and relevant to them? And, although this may sound basic, make sure your site tells visitors who you are and what you do. Finally, don't forget to wrap up each page with a strong "call to action" in which you tell prospects what to do next. For example, ask them to "Call for a free consultation!" or "Fill out our contact form to get more information," or "Click here to check out our portfolio." You need to prompt them to take further action.

Once you've written your website text, put it aside for a few days. Then look at it with fresh eyes, pass it around to a few friends, and make some tweaks. Then, be sure it gets a good proofreading. (Again, this is an opportunity to hire a pro. Typos on a website will give prospects a sloppy, negative image of your company.) Consider your website a work in progress. A great website is your best marketing bet, so take the time to do it right. Review it every four to six months to make sure it still tells your story in a relevant, compelling, accurate manner.

social media marketing

Social media websites are full-of-potential marketing tools. Put simply, "social media" is an organic online conversation. These conversations might take place on social networking sites (like Facebook and Google+), business networking sites (like LinkedIn), blogs (like WordPress and Blogger), microblogs (like Twitter), image-based sites (like Pinterest and Instagram), message boards/listservs, and a variety of other up-and-coming sites.

You — as a small business owner — will likely also use social media to showcase your expertise, connect with others in your industry, and meet like-minded people across the globe. Luckily, social media marketing is easy to try out, at your own pace.

While Facebook still holds the top social media spot, others (like YouTube, Instagram, Twitter, and Pinterest) are hot on its heels. Take some time to find the right ones for you. And don't forget the power of chat rooms and listservs. You can contribute your thoughts without the commitment of maintaining an actual page on a site.

Don't be afraid to tell people about your personal life, in moderation. People buy from those they know, like, and trust. Remember that your readers want relevant information. They want to hear about great new products that you recommend. They want tips. They want links to helpful articles and websites. You can also share timely information, such as promoting your current special offers and contests.

Once you get started with social media marketing, be consistent with your post frequency. Decide how many hours per week you'll spend updating your sites. Remember to contribute frequently when visiting other people's sites. This gets your name out there and establishes you as an expert in your field.

Don't forget to set some goals for your social media efforts. Do you want to increase web traffic to your company website? Then point your readers to select pages on your site. Do you want to showcase yourself as an expert? Then link to articles you've written. Do you want to promote your products, services, or events? Then share information and testimonials about them to help turn "lookers" into "buyers."

You're investing precious time in social media marketing, so define "results" for your business. Every few months, evaluate your social media marketing success. You can easily track website traffic by placing a counter on your site. You can analyze sales figures to see if they increase once you start blogging. You can check your ezine subscribers numbers to see if they increase once you start Tweeting. Simply look at your list of goals, and track both the quantifiable and anecdotal results.

free media coverage in publications

As small business owners, one of our marketing goals is to get our company names out there. But because many small businesses have limited budgets, we often can't afford traditional advertising methods in print media, radio, and television. So we need to rely on publicity. Both advertising and publicity offer great visibility within your community, but you have to pay for advertising. You get complete control of the message, but potential clients could be skeptical about your advertising claims. Publicity, on the other hand, is free. And it tends to have greater credibility because viewers feel that the content is prepared by objective television, radio, or newspaper editors.

You can have a reporter write an article about you and your services (which is especially great if you're one of the first professional organizers in your area, or if you have a unique niche). Or you can submit articles you've written on a variety of organizing topics. (You aren't necessarily looking to get paid for these articles; rather, the hope that a byline and contact information within the article will drive potential clients your way.) Either way, it won't cost you a dime and could get the phone ringing. If you write your own articles, consider providing tips relevant to a specific organizing holiday (see Appendix B for a list).

Getting publicity starts with a pitch letter or press release. Don't be scared off by the terminology. These are simply letters sent to the media with the intent of sharing information about your product or service. To craft your own press release or pitch letter, follow these four steps.

STEP 1: FIND YOUR PUBLICATION
Location, location, location! You've heard that before, and it DOES apply to publicity. Think of your target market, and then determine what they are reading, watching, and viewing on the internet. Is your niche moms and families? Check out some kid-focused publications. Do you help busy professionals organize their space or increase productivity? Zero in on local business journals.

Of course, your local newspaper will apply to just about every target market, and you should certainly include it in your list of potential media sources. But don't forget the smaller, more targeted publications. You'll often find a few freebie magazines or newspapers in a rack at your favorite cafe or sandwich shop. You could check online to find e-newsletters and blogs that are read by your target audience. And you could even go one step further by checking out the resources listed within these publications. You may find some media sources that you didn't even know about that could be a perfect match for your products or services! Start small and don't discount how valuable that coverage can be. It can often lead to bigger publications and exposure.

STEP 2: TARGET YOUR MESSAGE

So why should a newspaper, magazine, or news show give you exposure? That's your job to figure out! Think like their readers or viewers. What are they interested in? How would your product or service make their lives easier or better? What are you offering that is new or exciting? Even if you think your services are old news, you can spin them to complement something new and current. If your idea seems interesting to the journalist who reads it, you can count on seeing your name in the media soon!

If you're a relatively recent start-up and you're the town's first professional organizer, you might pitch the article as, "Local Woman Starts Professional Organizing Business" or "Springfield Man Craves Your Clutter." As our industry grows, so does public awareness. People are curious to learn about your locally-offered services. If you're working with a unique segment of the population (such as teaching high school students to organize their lockers and backpacks), or have a new approach to solving an old problem, this is news! We all have our niches, so capitalize on them! Likewise, if you develop a new product or service or reach a major milestone (such as your ten-year anniversary), this is news.

Perhaps you can tie your services in with a national trend. Just read your daily paper and watch the evening news for ideas. You might also take the angle of highlighting an upcoming organizing holiday. Check out "Chase's Calendar of Events" at your local library. It includes everything from "National Clean Out Your Refrigerator Month" to "Clutter Awareness Week." Or, simply capitalize on the season, such as goal setting in January or getting rid of garage clutter in the spring. Or, if you're offering a series of workshops or seminars, tie them in with an organizing holiday or seasonal holiday. This is news!

STEP 3: WRITE AND SEND THE MESSAGE

The press release and pitch letter are very similar, but the pitch letter is a little less formal and more conversational, written in the first person. It's a chance to "speak" to the journalist conversationally.

You can find contact names and email addresses on the inside front cover of most publications or on their websites. You should send press releases via email. It's worth noting that many editors don't like opening attachments, so text within emails are a better option.

If you don't hear back from the editor within a week or so, be sure to follow up with a phone call. It is very likely the press release fell to the bottom of the pile and she simply forgot or didn't get to it yet! Don't feel intimidated or that you're "bothering" him/her. According to the Public Relations Society of America, approximately 80% of news stories are generated by outside sources (like you)! Newspapers and other media depend on the general public to tell them what's going on in their communities.

STEP 4: BE PREPARED

Reporters often wait until the last minute to get going on a story, so don't be surprised to receive a phone call requesting an interview right then and there. Try to be available and flexible. You might want to prepare some information ahead of time so your answers will flow smoothly. What questions might the reporter ask you? Answer them on paper and you'll likely breeze through any interview. And remember, when you speak with a reporter, be yourself!

You can use this method of press release writing to reach any medium — newspaper, magazine, television, radio, or online publications — but it might be helpful to start with local print media to get your feet wet. It's much easier to "think on your feet" with the smaller publications, rather than on live radio or television or for larger-scale print publications. Save that for your next try at mastering the media.

See how easy publicity can be? If you're still not sure if writing a press release or pitch letter is worth your time, consider this: A 1/3 page ad in Real Simple magazine will run you nearly $107,000. A write-up about your cool new product that is a great fit for its readers: free and priceless!

TIP: Have a short list of organizing tips available to share with reporters. Newspapers love quick, easy bullet-points. You may also wish to gather some national statistics on disorganization or clutter. And if you have a newsletter, ask the reporter to include an offer for a free subscription at the end of the article. What a great way to build your database with people interested in your services! Before you finish the interview, confirm the spelling of your name and business, and ask them to include some contact information. When the article hits the press, you may be surprised how many calls you receive.

Now that you've made this great contact, put it on your calendar to keep in touch quarterly. Free publicity is as close as your friendly journalist! Follow her articles, and comment on her stories if you can tie them in with your area of expertise. Get to know the columns and publications that your target market reads. You never know when an opportunity will present itself.

PITCH IDEAS

Just keep your target market in mind when pondering what would interest them. Here are a few ideas:

- You are starting a new business (especially great if you are the first in your area)
- You want to showcase what you do and have the media cover the process (think before and after)
- You started a clutter support group
- You are offering a local workshop or series of classes
- You are offering services to a unique segment of the population
- You have tips that relate to an upcoming organizing holiday or season
- You are celebrating an important business anniversary (5 or 10 years, etc.)
- You are offering a contest
- You have created a new product
- You want to point out a trend or statistic or something timely

- You want to relate current news trends to how you can help its viewers/readers
- You have an interesting case study of a client or a before & after story

referral programs

Create an incentive program for current clients to encourage them to refer their family, friends, and co-workers to you. Be sure to offer a referral gift (such as a free hour of organizing or a gift certificate to a local store) so your "referees" find benefits in advocating for you. Don't overlook your "friends and family" contact list. They'll probably be happy to offer you referrals! Make sure all your family and friends know what you do, the type of client you most desire, and that you're currently taking on new clients. Also consider developing a cross-referral program with a complementary business, such as a housecleaner, Realtor, feng shui practitioner, or life coach.

speaking engagements

Speaking is a great way to get your name out there, showcase your expertise, and directly connect with people who need your services. Contact local mom's clubs, early childhood education centers, community education programs, elementary schools, church groups, senior centers, community centers, Rotary clubs, Chambers of Commerce, and local businesses to see if they'd like to have you speak. Sometimes offering free speaking engagements is a great way to build your database and get your name out. As you polish your speaking skills, you'll be able to command a higher rate for each presentation. Be sure to look for groups that fit your target market. For example, if you love to work with families, a local mom's group would be perfect. If you'd like to help senior citizens, develop a relationship with a senior complex or assisted living facility. Make sure the information and tips you present are relevant to your audience.

TIP: Get permission to sell organizing products and books after your presentation if you want to make a little extra money. Always have participants fill out a survey afterward, so you can improve with each speaking engagement. And, most importantly, be sure to collect the participants' names and email addresses so you can send occasional e-communications to stay in touch. (Always ask permission first by saying, "Please add your contact information to my sign-up sheet so you can receive free quarterly organizing tips and special discount offers," or something to that effect.)

---

other helpful marketing tactics

EXPOS AND TRADE SHOWS

Having a booth at a small business conference and expo might be a great opportunity to meet potential clients and market your services. If you want to have a booth at an expo or trade show, make sure its target market is your target market. Take the fee and your time into consideration when deciding which (if any) expos you'll attend. Make sure you have a way to capture contact information for everyone who passes through your booth. Consider offering a drawing for a free organizing session or invite passers-by to sign up for your free newsletter or ezine.

TESTIMONIALS AND REFERENCES

If you had an especially motivating and positive client session(s), consider asking for a written testimonial. Nothing speaks more highly of you than a satisfied client! You can take a few awesome client endorsements and use them in a variety of ways: post them on your website, use them in your brochure, or put them in your portfolio or media kit. It's also reassuring to have something prepared when potential clients ask for references.

It can be intimidating to ask for testimonials from your clients. But a satisfied client will nearly always be willing and happy to write one. The key is to ask in a timely manner. For example, when you're finishing a session and your client says, "Wow, you do amazing work," that is the perfect time to ask if they'd write you a short testimonial for use on your promotional materials. Or capture an endorsement by asking if you can quote someone when they rave about you. Another way to gather references is to hand out client feedback forms after your sessions or workshops, and be sure to include a spot for comments, as well as a checkbox that says, "You may use my comments for marketing purposes."

Don't be shy about asking for specific types of comments in your testimonials. Feel free to guide your clients a bit by encouraging them to share why they enjoyed working with you, the value they received from your services, how their lives have improved after your help, and why they would recommend you. That way, you don't end up with a generic and not-very-useful testimonial like, "Mary really did a great job." You want specifics, something with pow to tell potential clients that you're someone special — full of unique ideas, tons of skill, and a kind heart — who delivers value for money spent.

Make sure to attribute the testimonials to someone. Ask if you can use your client's name, the city of residence, and/or business name. Of course, an extremely disorganized person might feel some shame about hiring a professional organizer to straighten out his life. In those cases, just use your client's initials and the city of residence. Whatever you do, make sure you have your clients' permission to use their names. It's also nice to have the clients represent the target market you serve. For example, if you serve mainly corporate clients, be sure to include titles and company names of the clients served. That may impress prospects. Or if you want to work with families, see if you can work in details about the family in the quote, like "mother of five" or "stay-at-home dad."

Give testimonials a try. They are an amazing tool to show your expertise and bring in new clients without spending a cent.

marketing conclusion

Commit to developing a marketing plan. It is essential to a successful business! You've probably heard the saying, "Do what you love and the money will follow." It will, but you must have a plan and accountability. It will give you direction and provide a frame of reference as your business grows.

appendix A

frequently asked questions

frequently asked questions

When I coach prospective and new professional organizers, certain questions seem to pop up over and over. Here are some of them, because I'm sure you're wondering about them as well.

How long have you been a professional organizer?
I launched Time to Organize in 2000.

What prompted you to get into your line of work?
I was working at the University of Minnesota in a marketing position. Although I loved my job, I felt I was missing out on much of my then two-year-old son's life. So I began exploring other options. I began the process by writing down a list of my talents, skills, likes, and dislikes. I did some research online and talked to my mentors, friends, and family.

I think I first heard of the term "professional organizer" as I watched an episode of Oprah, when Julie Morgenstern was a guest. It then evolved from simple online research and talking with others to assessing my current skills and talents, and listening to my heart. I'd always wanted to own a business, and I desired a job that offered flexible hours. I attended a local NAPO meeting and, from there, a new career was launched! So, as you can see, my career exploration was pretty organic.

Could you please briefly outline the process of helping clients?
I start with a brief phone consultation to qualify them. (Will they be a good match for me and I for them?) At the first session, I spend anywhere from 30-60 minutes doing an assessment. Then we dig in for the remainder of the time (usually three hours per session). I work alongside them the entire time, coaching, teaching skills, setting up new systems, watching for fatigue, and encouraging them. When we wrap up, I offer homework assignments if they want to work on them between sessions on their own. It gives them accountability and gets the project done faster.

How do you handle assessments?
There are many ways to conduct assessments. (See the "Assessment" section of this book for full details.) Personally, I like to wrap the assessment and a work session together, so that I'm not providing free assessments and so that clients can see immediate results the very first time they meet me. But I have no problem with a new professional organizer offering a free, separate assessment or an established professional organizer charging for an in-depth assessment. It's a great way to get your foot in the door and to showcase your compassion, knowledge, and desire to help.

Generally, what portion of society do your customers come from — geographically, economically, and socially?
They come from all areas... mostly I accept clients who live close to me (within 30 miles) as a personal preference. They tend to be more suburban rather than in the city, maybe because I'm in a suburb, too. My target market is busy families. Economically, it's all over the place... I've had a few lower-income clients, some upper-income clients, and lots of middle-income clients. Those who really want to hire a professional organizer will usually find a way to afford it, even if they have to do some serious budgeting to fit it in. It's important for us, as professional organizers, to stress the value of our services. Our clients are learning skills from us that will last a lifetime.

When clients approach you, how open are they to let someone come into their life and change habits?
The clients are pretty open. If they're at the point that they're calling me, they feel pretty comfortable sharing the intimate details of their homes and offices with me. Although I know a lot of people think about calling an organizer, it often takes a while to actually make the call. I've had people say, "I saw your article in the paper," and then I realize it was from a year ago! I always phone-screen my clients so that they know I am coming in to transfer organizing skills to them. I don't accept clients who just want me act like a glorified housecleaner. They must be willing and open to new ideas and want to learn. I think there is some shame, especially in very messy homes or those who lose stuff frequently... they think they should be able to handle life on their own, but can't. I quickly reassure them that it's okay, nothing will surprise me, and that I don't judge. It is not a character flaw to be disorganized.

How many of your clients would you consider "hoarders" or "chronically disorganized" versus simply having too much stuff?
I've discovered all levels of disorganization. I've worked with a few hoarders (although they are not my target market), a number of chronically disorganized people, and a scattering of people who really didn't need an organizer at all! But most clients fall somewhere in the middle — they have some clutter issues, space issues, or just a lack of basic organizing skills. I would guess that about 75% of the time, clients have too much stuff that they're not using, loving, or needing. There are lots of psychological issues that go along with being cluttered, such as holding on to memories, hiding behind clutter, and feeling a need for physical abundance. It is my job to try to see those issues and gently support and guide the client.

How do you handle the huge over-abundance issue in our society?
In my opinion, this country is insanely purchase-crazy, materialistic, and over-abundant! Once my clients' stuff is organized, they tend to buy less. (They can actually see and find what they have.) I try to teach new rules, such as the "in/out" rule, such as if they buy a new pair of shoes, they must throw out or donate one old pair so they maintain their current amount. I try to get them to opt out of junk mail lists and credit card lists. I sometimes recommend they cancel magazine subscriptions if they seem to have more than they can comfortably read in a month, as well catalogs. But I try not to be pushy in this area, even though I feel passionate about it. I also stress how clients can save time and money by purchasing less.

Do you ever consult clients regarding their financial habits?
Not unless they ask, or if they've been a client for a long time. I've had clients ask for referrals for financial planners and debt counselors, so I help find them one.

How often do you recommend that clients purchase storage containers to aid in organization?
If they ask for recommendations, I give them. Usually, a lack of storage containers is not the problem. Of course, there are some fabulous organizing products out there, and they do make organizing so much more fun for both me and my clients. But I always work within my clients' budgets and first try to use what they already own. I always bring my label maker, using it when it feels "right." I am frequently asked which brand is best, and I think there are many fine models out there. I've used a Casio that lasted a long time. I currently have a Dymo LetraTag that is easy to use. The Brother P-Touch is also highly recommended by my peers.

What if a client cancels last-minute or isn't there when I arrive?
Realize that a no-show may be the result of a family emergency, so be understanding if this is the case and waive the fee if you feel obliged. I'll never forget the time I drove nearly 50 miles on a 90-degree day, seven months' pregnant — to arrive to a no-show client! I was so angry (and hot!), but I remembered my cancellation policy and felt better knowing that I'd at least recoup my gas and travel time expense. Later, I found out the client's daughter was taken to the emergency room just 30 minutes before our scheduled session, so I mellowed out, suspended my cancellation policy, and rescheduled with her.

Why does society need help to get organized?
We are in demand because not all people are born organized. No one teaches organizing skills in school. Parents are not transferring organizing skills to their kids. People buy too much stuff they don't need, and people hold on to stuff for the wrong reasons. Professional organizers can come in and coach, guide, and support. We're great listeners, amazing teachers, and wonderful resources.

Why is the industry of professional organizing growing so rapidly?
In 1995, there were a mere 834 members of NAPO. Within five years, that number grew to 1,358. Now, there are over 3,500! Our field is growing because it is a relatively easy and flexible business to launch. Professional organizing attracts job seekers from a variety of other fields, such as psychology, teaching, and event planning. And the topic of "organizing" has become mainstream, so the career of professional organizing is more understood.

How much should I charge?
The rate you charge depends on where you live (rural, urban, suburban), what type of organizing you're doing, and how long you've been organizing. I would caution against setting your fee too low. Many newer organizers don't think they're worthy of the standard organizing fees, which is a huge misnomer. I usually recommend at least $40 - $50 per hour for brand-new organizers, but that will vary depending upon the factors listed above. Rates nationally vary from $40 to over $200 per hour.

Should I worry about a sluggish economy?
The thought of starting a new business venture is scary at any time, but especially when an economy is sluggish. I'm frequently asked, "Is there enough business to go around? Will people purchase my services?" My answer is that people will always find money to buy what is important to them. If they truly want to get organized, they will find a way to do it. But it's up to you to share the benefits of getting organized. When times are tough financially, people are spending more time at home with their families, so their spaces need to be organized, neat, and comfortable. Also, the same amount of money is still floating around. It's just in different places and different people's wallets. Who has money right now, and can you find a way to work with that segment of the population?

Do you recommend hourly or project-based rates?
Personally, I offer only hourly rates and package deals. I know other organizers who offer project-based rates. I don't think one method is better than the other, and the decision is personal. However, for new organizers, I would only recommend hourly or session rates. It's really hard to gauge how long it will take to complete an organizing project until you have lots of experience under your belt. Even with years of experience, I still find this difficult. I could tell you — practically down to the minute — how long it would take me to organize a space. But when clients are involved (which they usually are), it throws in a whole new set of variables. How long does it take them to make decisions? How quickly can they identify each item when I ask, "What is this and how do you use it?" Are they prone to distractions? How do they deal with interruptions? Do they tire easily? Will they want to chat the entire time and tell me their life's stories? I recommend you opt for hourly rates at least for the first year of your new career.

Do you offer apprenticeships?
Personally, I do not. There are many reasons for this. The most important is the comfort levels of my clients. They are often embarrassed or ashamed of their current state of disorganization, so I don't want to add to their discomfort by bringing in yet another stranger to view it. (Equate it to when you go to the doctor and you're asked, "Is it all right if our intern sits in on the exam?" Yuck! It's embarrassing enough to have one person looking at you, but to have yet another person scrutinizing you and your "problems" might be too much.) However, it doesn't hurt to ask members of your local chapter of NAPO to see if someone in your area is looking for an assistant on larger jobs. You might also consider offering to pay an accomplished organizer his/her normal fee just to see him/her in action.

Do you offer gift certificates?
Yes, but with a caveat. I always first ask the potential buyer if the recipient of the gift certificate wants this type of gift. It's not a gift if the person on the receiving end is going to hate it or feel insulted by it. If you donate gift certificates to a local charity auction, remember that you can get a tax write-off for products but not for services. I recommend donating gift certificates only to auctions, not to raffles. (Again, ensuring your services go to a person who actually wants them.) And make sure gift certificates have an expiration date if allowed by your state (one year is good) and a mileage limit.

appendix B

small business resources

•

national organizing holidays

•

organizing product stores

•

donation resources

small business resources

American Institute of Certified Public Accountants 360 Degrees of Financial Literacy: Click on the "entrepreneurs" section to read articles including benefit and retirement plans, business insurance, business planning basics, advertising, business deductions, partnerships, and much more. Visit www.360financialliteracy.org.

Census Department Consumer Info: You'll find social, demographic and economic information. Visit www.census.gov.

Dreamstime.com: A favorite affordable source for stock photography to use on websites and brochures. Visit www.dreamstime.com.

Entrepreneur.com: Everything from free business forms to marketing, legal and success tips for home-based businesses and more. Visit www.entrepreneur.com.

FreeConferenceCalls.com: Set up free conference calls (bridge line) or teleclasses using these free services. Visit www.freeconferencecall.com or www.freeconference.com.

GoDaddy.com: Purchase your web domain names here for an affordable price — much lower than many of the other domain name providers. They also offer affordable website hosting services. Visit www.godaddy.com.

Google Voice: Offering some great free options, Google Voice is something to consider before you purchase a new phone or second phone line for your business. You can get a new number that rings on any or all of your current phones, online voicemail with transcription, and much more. Visit www.google.com/voice.

Internal Revenue Service: Small business and self-employed one-stop resource offering a broad range of resources, as well as industry/profession specific information for self-employed entrepreneurs, employers, and businesses. Includes a listing of deductible business expenses. Visit www.irs.gov.

Legal Shield: Available in 49 U.S. states and four Canadian provinces, this is a great money-saver if you think you'll be needing a lawyer in the upcoming year. You pay a flat-rate fee each month, and you'll have access to local lawyers as you need them. Visit www.legalshield.com for details.

Mail Chimp: Similar to the Constant Contact email management program, although not quite as robust. It does have a nice auto-responder feature. And, it is free! Visit www.mailchimp.com.

National Association of Women Business Owners: The National Association of Women Business Owners is a dues-based national organization representing the interests of women entrepreneurs across all industries. Find a chapter near you or view its online business resource center by visiting www.nawbo.org.

Pay Pal: Set up a merchant account for free and accept credit card payment via your website or their credit card reader with a few simple steps. They'll take about a three percent commission, which is much less than you'd pay if you opened a merchant account with a major credit card company. Visit www.paypal.com.

SCORE: Get free, confidential small business advice from a business professional via email or in person. Locate a Service Corps of Retired Executives (SCORE) counselor near you for free counseling services. Plus view how-to articles and business templates. Visit www.score.org.

Secretary of State's Office: Search the internet for "Secretary of State" and your state's name.

Small Business Administration: For up-to-the-minute info about government data and services for small businesses, visit www.sba.gov. You'll find helpful publications and sample business plans.

Square: Accept credit card payments using this small device that plugs into your smartphone or iPad (with internet connection) so you can swipe and instantly process clients' credit cards. You pay a small fee per transaction and funds are sent to your checking account within 24 hours. Visit www.squareup.com.

Toastmasters: Great resource to improve your public speaking. Find a local chapter near you at www.toastmasters.org.

United States Patent and Trade Office: Helpful information regarding trademarks, service marks, copyrights, and patents. This is where you'd go to register your company name if you want to own it exclusively on a national level. Visit www.uspto.gov.

Vistaprint.com: This is an affordable option for printing your first set of business cards when your funds are low and the details of your business (specialty, business name, website address, etc.) are not yet set in stone. Visit www.vistaprint.com.

Womenowned.com: View hundreds of articles, access business tools and resources, build your own online network, write your own blog, sell products and services, and share with other members. Visit www.womanowned.com.

national organizing holidays

Use this list to remind yourself of great promotional opportunities throughout the year. These special days are a wonderful opportunity to contact your local media and tell them about any upcoming holidays, with the offer to share organizing tips with their readers/viewers.

JANUARY
Get Organized Month
Be On Purpose Month
Clean Out Your Closets Month
Clean Off Your Desk Day: Second Monday in January

FEBRUARY
Archive Your Files Month
Pay Your Bills Week: Third week in February
Clean Out Your Computer Day: Second Monday in February
Valentine's Day: February 14

MARCH
Organize Your Home Office Day: Second Tuesday in March
Procrastination Week: Second week of March
Clutter Awareness Week: Third week of March
Clean Out Your Closet Week: Third week of March

APRIL
Stress-Awareness Month
Tax Day: April 15
Organize Your Files Week: Third week of April
National TV-Free Week: Fourth week of April
Administrative Professionals Week: Last week of April

MAY
Moving Month
Scrapbook Month
Revise Your Work Schedule Month
Mother's Day: Second Sunday in May

JUNE
Father's Day: Third Sunday in June
Small Business Week: Second Week in June

JULY
Purposeful Parenting Month
Financial Freedom Day: July 1
Take Charge of Change Week: First week of July

AUGUST
Professional Speakers Month
Simplify Your Life Week: First week of August

SEPTEMBER
ADD/ADHD Month
Self-Improvement Month
Back-To-School Time
Fight Procrastination Day: First Wednesday in September

OCTOBER
Kitchen and Bath Month
Computer Learning Month
Medical Information Month
Home-Based Business Week: Second week in October
Take Back Your Time Day: October 24

NOVEMBER
Addictions Month
Clean Out Your Refrigerator Month
Pursuit of Happiness Week: Second week in November
Buy Nothing Day: The day after Thanksgiving
America Recycles Day: November 15

DECEMBER
Stress-Free Holidays Month
Make Up Your Mind Day: December 31

organizing product stores

GENERAL SUPPLIES
Ikea: www.ikea.com
Target: www.target.com
Walmart: www.walmart.com

GENERAL OFFICE SUPPLIES
Avery: www.avery.com
Office Depot: www.officedepot.com
Quill: www.quill.com
Staples: www.staples.com

UNIQUE AND BEAUTIFUL OFFICE SUPPLIES
Levenger: www.levenger.com
russell + hazel: www.russellandhazel.com
See Jane Work: www.seejanework.com

HOME IMPROVEMENT/CLOSETS
California Closets: www.californiaclosets.com
Easy Closets: www.easyclosets.com
Home Depot: www.homedepot.com
Lowe's: www.lowes.com

ORGANIZING PRODUCTS
Bed, Bath & Beyond: www.bedbathandbeyond.com
The Container Store: www.containerstore.com
Cost Plus World Market: www.worldmarket.com
Crate & Barrel: www.crateandbarrel.com
CB2: www.cb2.com
Current: www.currentcatalog.com
Linens-n-Things: www.lnt.com
Organized A to Z: www.organizedatoz.com
Organize-It: www.organizeit.com
Pottery Barn: www.potterybarn.com
Rubbermaid: www.rubbermaid.com
Solutions: www.solutions.com
Storables: www.storables.com
Umbra: www.umbra.com

donation resources

Please note that not every donation resource listed will be available in your area. Do an online search to see if one exists in your area. Visit the websites listed to find locations near you. Or try typing in the organization's name and your state or city into your favorite search engine, like Google or Yahoo.

HOUSEHOLD ITEMS

- Goodwill accepts furniture, cars, clothing, books, toys and more. Visit www.goodwill.org/locator to find a location near you.

- Disabled Vietnam Veterans accepts clothing, housewares, and some furniture. Neighborhood pick-ups available in some areas. Visit www.vva.org.

- Lupus Foundation accepts clothing, housewares, some furniture. Neighborhood pick-ups available in some areas. Visit www.lupuspickup.org and click on "chapter locator."

- Catholic Charities accepts personal care items like blankets, sheets, gloves, shoes, and socks. Also furniture; no clothing. Visit www.catholiccharitiesusa.org.

- Salvation Army accepts clothing, housewares. Visit www.satruck.com to schedule a pick-up.

- Epilepsy Foundation accepts most household items (clothing, shoes, bedding items, housewares, toys, games, tools, and small appliances) and will often pick up at your home. Visit www.epilepsyfoundation.org.

CLOTHING ONLY

- Many local organizations provide low-income women with gently used clothing suitable for interviews and the workplace. Try typing "donate business clothing" and your state or city into Yahoo or Google.

EYEGLASSES

- Lens Crafters, Pearle Vision, Sears Optical, Target Optical, BJ's, and Sunglass Hut all accept used eyeglasses. Local Lions Clubs also accept glasses.

CARS

- Try www.donateacar.com or www.donate-car-for-charity.com. There are also many local charities that accept vehicles.

CELL PHONES

- Best Buy provides free and easy recycling of any brand of cell phone.
- Target stores provide free and easy recycling of any brand of cell phone.
- The AT&T Wireless Reuse & Recycle Program accepts free drop-offs of all brands of unwanted cell phones and accessories at AT&T Wireless retail stores.
- Sprint Project Connect offers free drop-off of all brands of wireless phones at Sprint Stores.
- Staples office supply stores offer free drop-off recycling services for used cell phones.
- Through the Verizon Wireless HopeLine Phone Recycling Program, consumers get free drop-off recycling services for used cell phones at retail store locations.
- Many local schools accept cell phones as a fundraiser.
- Sell old cell phones at www.Gazelle.com. Simply answer a few questions about the model and condition of the phone, ship it for free, and collect your payment.

ART PROJECTS

- Try your local Parks and Recreation Department and local elementary schools to donate anything that could be used for art projects for children. Also, try your local museums.
- Magazines can be donated to schools, nursing homes, or other art programs. (Be sure to remove address labels first.)

ENVIRONMENTAL RESOURCES FOR RECYCLING

- Freecycle Network is similar to eBay, but no money is exchanged because you are giving what you no longer want to someone who needs or wants it. Visit www.freecycle.org.
- Rethink Recycling is a great place to learn how to reduce garbage and increase recycling. Visit www.rethinkrecycling.com.

GETTING RID OF JUNK MAIL AND TELEMARKETING PHONE CALLS

- Reduce the hail of unwanted junk mail by contacting the Direct Marketing Association to remove your name from mailing lists. Call 212-768-7277 or visit www.dmachoice.org.
- Opt out of receiving paper catalogs at one convenient website. Visit www.catalogchoice.org.

- Stop the flow of credit cards offers. Visit www.optoutprescreen.com to stop credit bureaus from selling your information to banks or credit card companies. (You'll have to provide your Social Security Number.)

- Stop unwanted telemarketing phone calls by adding phone numbers to the Do Not Call Registry. Call1-888-382-1222 or visit www.donotcall.gov. (Must have an active email address to register online).

GETTING RID OF HOUSEHOLD HAZARDOUS WASTE

- For information, contact the county in which you live.

WHEN YOU NEED TO GET RID OF A DUMPSTER-FULL OR MORE

- Bagster: Pick up a Bagster bag at your local home improvement store. It's simple to set up and strong enough to hold up to 3,300 lb of debris or waste. Schedule the collection online or by phone, and the filled bag will be picked up within a day or two. This is often less expensive than a traditional dumpster. Visit www.thebagster.com to learn more.

- TUBS, Inc: Visit www.tubsinc.com or type "dumpster" or "garbage removal" plus your state or city into Yahoo or Google to find other local removal services.

- 1-800-GOT-JUNK: North America's largest junk removal service. They do all the loading into their truck, and then your junk is recycled, taken to a transfer station, or sent to a landfill. Pricing is based on your city, the volume of material, and the nature of your material. They'll take construction materials, garden waste, furniture, appliances, and other items. No hazardous waste accepted. Visit www.1800gotjunk.com or call 1-800-got-junk.

appendix C

sample press releases & pitch letter

•

sample announcement letter

•

sample basic assessment form

•

sample marketing timeline

•

sample coupons and invoice

sample press release #1

FOR IMMEDIATE RELEASE:

Contact: Suzy Entrepreneur, Professional Organizer
Suzy's Organizing Emporium
651/555-1244 (cell)
suzy@organizingemporium.com (email)

Clutter Attack: The Third Week of March is National Clutter Awareness Week

Neatnic City, Minnesota
March 1, 2017

Clutter Awareness Week, which is March 21 - 27, is a wake-up call to attack that clutter! Clutter might be as extensive as a basement full of old clothes, toys, papers, and furniture that you don't use. It can be as simple as a pile of magazines and junk mail that you'll never read. Whatever the amount of clutter, it causes stress. You can't find things when you need them. You know clutter affects your life, as well as the way people see you. So this week, stop contemplating your clutter and dedicate some time to conquer it!

If you have trouble getting started, enlist the help of a friend. Begin with a small area of the home or office: the bathroom cabinet, your purse or briefcase, your car, or one kitchen drawer. Relish in the sense of accomplishment you feel. Now, move on to larger areas. The hallway closet. Your office desk. The garage. As you clear clutter, let go of emotional baggage that you don't really need. Ask yourself, "Is this item beautiful, useful, or loved?" If not, get rid of it!

Tips for getting clutter free

- Before you buy, think about what's truly important to you. What brings you joy, satisfaction, and fulfillment? Try to look beyond the initial "thrill of the purchase" and see what provides deeper moments of meaning.

- Make concrete organization goals. Instead of saying, "I will get organized," say, "I will clean out two kitchen cupboards this weekend." Commit to spending a set amount of time each week on conquering clutter, even if it's just half an hour.

- Make yourself accountable. Tell a friend or family member of your goals. Write them down. Paste them to your bathroom mirror or refrigerator so you see them every morning.

A free quarterly organizing tips newsletter is available from Suzy's Organizing Emporium by calling 651-555-1234. More tips available at www.organizingemporium.com

Whether clients are looking for new ways to save time at home or in the office, or they need someone to help declutter their house or desk, Suzy's Organizing Emporium can coach clients to ensure the process of purging, organizing, and placing household and office essentials makes sense. Weekly "Keep it Simple" support groups and organizing workshops are also available.

# # #

If you'd like more information about this topic, or to schedule an interview with Suzy Entrepreneur, please call 651/555-1234 or e-mail suzy@organizingemporium.com.

sample press release #2

FOR IMMEDIATE RELEASE:

Contact: Suzy Entrepreneur, Professional Organizer
Suzy's Organizing Emporium
651/555-1244 (cell)
suzy@organizingemporium.com (email)

Neatnic-City Woman Finds Her Passion in Clutter

Neatnic City, Minnesota
August 15, 2017

Susy Entrepreneur has finally found her passion — in other people's clutter. This Neatnic-City woman recently launched a new company, Suzy's Organizing Emporium, which guides the organizationally-challenged to simplify their lives, declutter their homes, and find time for themselves. Her weekly "Keep it Simple" support group also helps local residents learn tips and tricks to rid themselves of time, space, and energy-zapping clutter in a non-threatening, light-hearted environment.

If you'd like to learn more about getting organized, Suzy's Organizing Emporium is sponsoring a "Conquer Your Clutter" workshop on Thursday, August 31, from 7:00 p.m.-8:30 p.m. at the Neatnic-City Community Center. To pre-register, call 651/555-1234. Cost is $25 per person.

Suzy's Organizing Emporium, a Neatnic City-based organizing business, offers the following time management and simplicity tips to help individuals make a difference in their own lives.

- Know your biological rhythms. Some people flourish in the mornings, while others do their best in the afternoons or evenings. When you're at your best, organize top-priority projects and those that require lots of concentration.
- If you're trying to get (and stay) organized, actually pencil in "appointments" with yourself to do specific projects.
- Try the five-minute rule. Immediately take care of any tasks that you can finish in five minutes or less, rather than putting them off till later: mail a letter, mark a date on the calendar, sign a document, put away the laundry.
- Try to simplify the material possessions in your life. Before you buy, ask yourself if you really need it. Remember, you'll have to find a place for it, clean it, and maintain it.

Whether clients are looking for new ways to save time at home or in the office, or they need someone to help declutter their house or desk, Suzy's Organizing Emporium can coach clients to ensure the process of purging, organizing, and placing household and office essentials makes sense. Suzy's Organizing Emporium president, Suzy Entrepreneur, stresses that "all clients' needs are unique, so each organization project is tailored to help them be most efficient." Weekly "Keep it Simple" support groups and organizing workshops are also available.

# # #

If you'd like more information about this topic, or to schedule an interview with Suzy Entrepreneur, please call 651/555-1234 or e-mail suzy@organizingemporium.com.

sample pitch letter

[E-MAIL SUBJECT LINE:]
Do you have 36 hours' worth of work on your desk?

September 15, 2017
Dear Ms. Smith,

Did you know that the average desk worker has 36 hours of work on his or her desk and spends three hours per week sorting piles trying to find the project to work on next?

Suzy's Organizing Emporium intends to ease that pile by teaching innovative organizing techniques through a series of four weekly Get Your Office in Order workshops. They are designed to give home-based business owners the skills and techniques needed to make their businesses run more efficiently. And because we know that time is tight for these folks, each workshop will be jam-packed with information in a short, 45-minute Lunch N Learn format. Box lunches will be provided!

With National Home-Based Business Week coming up the second week of October, I think your business section readers will enjoy learning about this series of Get Your Office in Order workshops. If you'd like to learn more about the workshop series or how getting organized can increase productivity, lower stress, and increase income for small business owners, please call or e-mail me.

Sincerely,

Suzy Entrepreneur, Professional Organizer
Suzy's Organizing Emporium

651/555-1234 (office)
651/555-1244 (cell)
suzy@organizingemporium.com (email)
www.organizingemporium.com (website)

sample announcement letter

[INSERT DATE HERE]

Dear [INSERT NAME HERE]

I am embarking upon a new journey and want to share my news with you!

I have decided to open my own professional organizing business, called [INSERT COMPANY NAME HERE]. As a professional organizer, I will help clients eliminate clutter, maximize available space, learn new organizing skills, and develop time-saving systems for [HOME/OFFICE].

Did you know that the average person loses an hour a day due to disorganization? As you encounter people who are living amidst overstuffed filing cabinets, disastrous closets, and chaotic kitchens, please give them my business card. By getting — and staying — organized, they will save valuable time each day by being able to easily locate items in their homes and offices.

I will be serving the [INSERT CITY/AREA YOU WILL SERVE] area and will be working [PART-TIME/FULL TIME/DAYS OR TIMES AVAILABLE TO WORK]. I would especially like to work with [INSERT DESIRED CLIENTELE], so if you can pass along my name to anyone who fits this description, I'd really appreciate it!

I welcome any advice you might have for a new small business owner, and I look forward to keeping you up to date on my new venture!

Warmest regards,

[INSERT YOUR NAME AND SIGNATURE HERE]
[ENCLOSE 5 BUSINESS CARDS, BROCHURE IF AVAILABLE]

sample basic assessment form

Name ____

Phone ________________________ Cell ________________________________

Email____

Address ____________________________ City ____________ Zip __________

Today's date ____________ Session booked? ____________________________

What are your areas of concern? (Circle all that apply.)

home office mail time management filing system kitchen bedroom

family room kids room basement living room garage craft room

other ____

Why do you want to get organized? What are your goals for this organizing project?

____

____

____

What are your organizational challenges?

____

____

____

What IS working well in your home/office?

____

____

____

What is NOT working well in your home/office?

____

____

____

What is the best time and day to meet? ______________________________

What is your deadline or timeframe? ________________________________

Do you have a budget in mind? ____________________________________

How did you find me? ____

marketing timeline

MONTH	MARKETING ACTIVITY	COST

sample coupons, invoice, gift certificate

SHARE WITH A FRIEND COUPON

Share this coupon with a friend and they will receive $50 off their first organizing session (3-hour minimum). And, as a bonus for you, when you refer a friend, you'll also receive $50 off your next session!

Who referred you? ____________________

Offer expires: ____________________

SAVE TIME! SAVE MONEY!

When you refer a friend who then becomes a client, you'll receive one FREE hour at your next organizing session!

Value: ____________________

Offer expires: ____________________

INVOICE/RECEIPT

Date:____________________

Service Provided: ____________________

________ hours @

$ ________ per hour = ____________________

Total: $ ____________________

Supplies: $ ____________________

Tax (if applicable): $ ____________________

Other: $ ____________________

Total due: $____________________

Thank you for your business. We appreciate referrals and love clients like you, so please tell your friends about us!

GIFT CERTIFICATE

GOOD FOR A THREE-HOUR ORGANIZING SESSION IN YOUR HOME!

Gifted To: ____________________

A Gift From: ____________________

Offer valid within the metro area. Please call xxx-xxx-xxxx to schedule.

Issue Date: ____________________ Offer Expires: ____________________

appendix D

8-week business jump-start plan

8-week business jump-start plan

You've read the book, and now you're excited and motivated to begin your new career as a professional organizer. But where to start? If you're ready to jump in, you can follow this 8-week business jump-start plan. In eight weeks, you can be up and running! Or, you may work at your own pace, either more quickly or slowly as your schedule allows. Check off each task as you complete it.

WEEK ONE

❒ **Decide on a business entity:** There are five main types of business formations, described in the "Choosing a Business Entity" section. Please consider consulting an attorney or tax accountant to guide you through this decision. You can also find helpful information at www.legalzoom.com, www.legalshield.com, and www.sba.gov.

❒ **Find your niche:** Do you have any ideas for a niche? Who do you want to help? What services do you feel comfortable offering? Take a minute to ask yourself, "How do I differentiate myself from others in my industry?" It's time to explore your uniqueness, with the ultimate goal of increasing sales and improving client relationships. In order to differentiate, you need to define your "choice clients." It's important to define a target market. Simply put, your target market is the people you most want to serve. Whether it's home-based business folks, stay-at-home moms, time-starved college students, downsizing senior citizens, or paper-crazed executives, knowing your target market will help you focus your marketing strategies on that group. You can't be all things to all people. As you ponder your choice clientele, you can think about demographics (such as age, sex, income, marital status, occupation), lifestyle (such as health-conscious, business-focused), and geographic location.

Who/what intrigues you the most? Start there! But don't close the door on other opportunities. You may find that an area you hadn't considered turns out to be your favorite type of job.

❒ **Start a local resource list:** Start compiling a list of local resources, such as handymen, closet installers, housecleaners, junk haulers, appraisers, psychologists, and life coaches, as well as local donation sites, consignment stores, and recycling sites. You'll appear professional, and your clients will appreciate your advice and recommendations. Type it up and laminate it, or make several copies to hand out as needed. Or simply keep the list handy on the smartphone, laptop, or tablet that you take to client visits.

Also, create a list of those who you need to contact to help get your business up and running (such as accountant, lawyer, graphic designer, web designer, etc.) You'll be glad to have this contact information organized and handy.

❒ **Educate yourself:** Read ONE book from the recommended reading list in the "Educational Resources" section of this book.

WEEK TWO

❒ **Select and register your company name**: Declaring your company name is an important first step. It makes this whole "new business idea" really official. There's no turning back now! So, start brainstorming about a company name. Take 30 minutes today to brainstorm. Grab a piece of paper, jot down every word or phrase that comes to mind, and then start mixing and matching for the perfect combination. Then use your thesaurus to discover new ways to say those words. (Try www.thesaurus.com.) It may be helpful to have a brainstorming party with friends or family. Invite them over for a fun evening of wordplay, which will hopefully result in your new company name.

Once you narrow down your favorite names to five or so, see if the names are available. (Follow the directions in the "Selecting a Company Name" section of this book.) If you need to register your company name with your local Secretary of State's office or County Register of Deeds Office, do that now as well.

❒ **Prepare your take-along bag**: Now is the time to prepare your take-along bag. This is fun! What you bring to client sessions will depend on the type of organizing you do. Review the suggested supply list in the "Preparing Your Take-Along Bag" section of this book.

❒ **Research insurance**: This week, research business insurance. Contact insurance agents in your area to find a policy that suits you. Make sure you give detailed information about the type of services you provide so that the policy will cover you fully. For example, you'll want to be covered if you or a client get hurt during or as a result of an organizing session, or if you accidentally break something. Also, you'll want to be covered in case a client accuses you of stealing or destroying his/her property. Take the time to fully discuss your needs with your agent. Get quotes from at least two agents. (If you know other professional organizers, ask them for recommendations to trusted agents.)

❒ **Understand your deductible expenses**: Whether you hire an accountant to do your taxes or you're the do-it-yourself type, it's important to understand the multitude of deductible business expenses available to the small business owner. Review the list in the "Record-Keeping" section of this book.

Also, start your financial record-keeping system at this time. Whether you use QuickBooks, Quicken, FreshBooks, Excel, or even a simple paper ledger, get it up and running now.

❒ **Educate yourself**: Take a field trip to a local office supply store, discount store, or organizing store (if you have one nearby) and scout out organizing products. Take note of products you've never seen before.

WEEK THREE

❒ **Set up shop:** Now is the time to set up your home office. Purchase your basic office supplies, arrange the office furniture in a functional manner, add some personality with a beautiful painting or potted plant — instant office!

❒ **This week, set up your phone system.** If you don't want to purchase a separate business line, you can use your home line, but make sure family members know to avoid answering any "unknown" calls. (Caller ID is a life-saver.) Another option is to use a cell phone for your business line. Or check out Google Voice!

❒ **Record your outgoing voicemail message.** You'll want to state your name and company name, and keep it brief. You could say something like this: "You have reached the office of ABC Organizing. Please leave a message for Susie Organizer and I'll call you back shortly."

If you'd like to keep your home address private, you may want to purchase a PO box to receive your mail. Set it up this week if you choose.

❒ **Consider NAPO membership:** Once you get the initial start-up equipment in place, your next business expense may be membership dues for the National Association of Productivity and Organizing Professionals (NAPO). Recognize that although the dues may seem expensive, you should consider them an investment in yourself and your business. NAPO dues are about $275 per year. You'll benefit from the education opportunities, listing in their online member directory, monthly newsletter, discussion forums and listserv, and so much more.

If you have a local chapter of NAPO within driving distance, please join this as well, or at least sign up to attend an upcoming meeting as a guest. It's a great way to meet other organizers, brainstorm, form new friendships, volunteer, and learn new skills.

❒ **Open a business checking account:** It's a good idea to keep your business checking and/or savings account separate from your personal bank account, so call a few local banks to inquire about their small business packages. (Some banks will give you a free checking account and even free checks. But they may not advertise these great deals, so be sure to ask.)

You might consider having a separate credit card account for business-related purchases as well. Research and compare credit card offers at www.nerdwallet.com.

❒ **Educate yourself:** Read ONE book from the recommended reading list in the "Educational Resources" section of this book.

WEEK FOUR

❒ **Create business cards:** Create some simple business cards. Print a small amount because your specialties and contact information may change as your business grows.

If your budget is small, consider the inexpensive business cards at www.vistaprint.com or www.moo.com. Or have cards made at your office supply store.

❒ **Start practicing:** It's important to get experience as a professional organizer. If you haven't already had this opportunity, now is the time to find someone in need of your services. You may need to offer them for free or at a discounted rate. That is okay! Think of friends, family members, acquaintances, former coworkers, or anyone you know who might like some help. Also, consider donating your time to organize at your favorite local charity... organize the supply room at church, the kitchen at a women's shelter, or whatever you can find. Just about every company could use some help.

List ten or more possible "practice" clients you could contact for a free (or cheap) session. Then, draft an announcement letter (see Appendix C for a Sample Announcement Letter) and send it out to the people and organizations on your list. Get a few practice sessions under your belt this month. Ask for a letter of recommendation at the end of your job. Start a portfolio of your work. Include photos of your past work. (Always ask clients' permission before taking "before and after" photos.)

❒ **Create a product portfolio:** It should contain pictures of organizing products that you can show your clients when describing product recommendations or storage ideas that might be helpful to them. This could be a 3-ring binder that you divide into areas of the home, or you could go digital on your laptop or tablet. Pinterest is also a great way to organize thoughts, ideas, and inspiration with regards to different areas of organizing! This will be a work in progress. Add to it frequently.

❒ **Educate yourself:** Take a trip to your local library and spend an hour or two skimming magazines for organizing articles. Make copies of any that intrigue you, and start an "ideas" file for your office.

WEEK FIVE

❒ **Practice your phone intake skills:** Are you ready for your phone to ring? Having a scripted phone conversation to follow may be helpful. Many organizers create an "intake form" to guide them through a series of questions for the potential client. Create a phone intake form this week, make copies, and keep them near the phone. If you don't want to create your own phone intake form, Time to Organize sells a great one. Order at www.timetoorganize.com/career. Have a friend practice with you. Try out your phone intake form to see if you get the information you need.

❒ **Create your client contract:** Once you book a session, it is helpful to mail clients a confirmation form/contract/agreement to detail the scheduled date(s) and time(s) of the session(s), your fee, your cancellation policies, and payment expectations. This week, create your own client contract. If you don't want to create your own, Time to Organize also sells a simple one-page client contract form. Order at www.timetoorganize.com/career.

❒ **Create your invoice/receipt:** At the end of each session, you'll need to collect payment for the day's work. Some clients would like a receipt of some sort. You can create your own invoice/receipt on your computer (just leave blanks to fill in at the end of the session, such as the number of hours worked, hourly rate, supplies purchased, etc.) or simply purchase a receipt book at your local office supply store. Either way is fine, but offering a receipt is professional and essential. Or, if you use a credit card reader (like Square) to accept payment, an email receipt will be automatically sent to your clients.

❒ **Set up your database:** You'll want to have some way to track clients and prospects as your business grows. This could be as simple as filling out client info on index cards and storing them in an index card box or setting up an easy filing system. Or, you could store contacts in a spreadsheet program like Excel. You might also consider a database program like Access, FileMaker Pro, Act!, or Salesforce. Any of these methods are fine, but just be sure to maintain good records and keep it up to date. Collect basic contact info about each client/prospect, such as name, address, phone number, and email address. You can also include pertinent information about each client and the sessions you've completed. Perhaps record their birthdays, favorite colors, pets and children's names, occupation, directions to their homes/offices, or anything else that might be useful.

❒ **Educate yourself:** Read ONE book from the recommended reading list in the "Educational Resources" section of this book.

WEEK SIX

❒ **Set income goals for this year:** Remember what you learned in the "Setting Your Fee" section of this book. Figure out a few salary scenarios. First, determine what you want to make annually, and then work backward to figure out how much you'll need to work weekly to attain that goal. This will help you figure out how much to charge per hour. Remember, these are the "billable hours" you'll work. This does not include the non-billable hours, such as doing administrative and marketing tasks.

Use this table to calculate your fee:

If you want to make $xx,xxx per year:

$xx,xxx divided by xx weeks per year = $xx per week

Now, how many billable hours can you work per week?
If you will work 20 billable hours per week, then you'll need to charge $xx per hour.
If you will work 15 billable hours per week, then you'll need to charge $xx per hour.
If you will work 10 billable hours per week, then you'll need to charge $xx per hour.
If you will work 6 billable hours per week, then you'll need to charge $xx per hour.

Also, think about how far you're willing to travel for clients and if you'll charge a travel fee for clients outside this range.

❒ **Educate yourself with teleclasses and workshops:** Learning organizing techniques from books is great, but nothing beats "in person" organizing education. See if your local community education department offers any workshops on organizing. They are usually quite inexpensive, taught by a local professional organizer, and a great opportunity to see a real PO in action. Be sure to introduce yourself as a new organizer. Maybe you'll make a new friend or mentor.

❒ **Take NAPO's teleclasses.** (NAPO members get a reduced rate, but the teleclasses are also open to the public.) Some include: Introduction to Professional Organizing, Starting an Organizing Business, Fundamental Organizing Principles, Starting Out as a Residential Organizer, Starting Out as a Business Organizer, Time Management, Fundamental Organizing Principles, and Chronic Disorganization. There is a fee for them (ranging from $45 - $299), but you'll find them very helpful, especially if you don't have any other educational opportunities in your area. (Members receive discounted pricing.) Register at www.napo.net.

❒ **Educate yourself:** Take a field trip to a local office supply store, discount store, or organizing store (if you have one nearby) and scout out organizing products. Take note of products you've never seen before.

WEEK SEVEN

❒ **Write a press release:** To get local media to put you in the spotlight, you'll need to let them know about your business. One of the easiest ways to do this is via a press release. Review the "Writing a Press Release or Pitch Letter" section of this book, and create your own to send to your local paper(s). For inspiration, review the "National Organizing Holidays" section of this book to see if you can tie into one coming up next month.After you write your press release, you need to actually send it! Then, follow up with the paper's editor a week later to see if it piqued his interest.

❒ **Create a physical safety plan:** Write up your personal safety plan. (See tips in the "Physical Safety Tips" section of this book.) Include what type of clients you will not work with. Set parameters to let a spouse/friend/partner know your whereabouts each day, and how you might get out of an uncomfortable situation should the need arise. Practice your "panic code" phone call or "get out" excuses.

❒ **Look into networking groups:** Investigate trade and business associations in your area that include a wide variety of professions. Contact your local Chamber of Commerce. Community service clubs, such as Rotary, Lions and Kiwanis Clubs, may also be helpful. Consider business networking groups such as Business Network Int'l (www.BNI.com) and the National Association of Women Business Owners (www.nawbo.com). Call a few, plan to attend some upcoming meetings as a guest, and select one to join if the fit seems right. Be able to introduce yourself and succinctly tell people what services you offer and how you can help them get organized.

❒ **Educate yourself:** Read ONE book from the recommended reading list in the "Educational Resources" section of this book.

WEEK EIGHT

❒ **Create a marketing timeline:** Review the "50 Ideas to Market Your Business" section in this book. Then, create a list of 10-15 marketing ideas you'd like to try. Next, fill in the Sample Marketing Timeline provided in Appendix C. On the timeline, you might also include business goals such as creating a follow-up program, liability issues, improving business skills, reviewing your expenses and revenue, and finally, etching out time for creating next year's marketing plan. Sound simple? It is! With a plan, you can get all those ideas out of your head and onto paper. You'll sleep better. Or create your own spreadsheet in Excel. It's easy to rearrange, redistribute, add, and delete with a tap of the keyboard.

❒ **Review income goals, get motivated, and get started:** You're almost there. This week, review the income goals you set in earlier. Take note of your weekly/monthly client session goals so you have something to work toward. You've come so far. The hard work is done. Now, you just need the confidence to move forward, put yourself out there, and find clients who need you! Remember, even though you're a beginner organizer, you know loads more than any client will know about organizing. Even though you're new to this business, you've probably been organizing all your life. Use your talents and make a difference in people's lives — starting today!

❒ **Educate yourself:** Take a trip to your local library and spend an hour or two skimming magazines for organizing articles. Make copies of any that intrigue you, and start an "ideas" file for your office.

conclusion

final thoughts

After reading through this book, are you even more intrigued about this amazing career? There are so many wonderful benefits. With such low start-up costs, it's easy to take a chance on something new. Be your own boss. Set your own hours. Find a niche you love. Make a real difference in people's lives. If you were born to organize, then follow your passion! When you can make money doing what you love, you'll be continually energized.

I took this leap of faith many years ago. I've never looked back or regretted a moment. Yes, there will be tough times, as you struggle to build your client base, balance your home/work lives, and "do it all." But the payoffs can be huge, not only in dollars but in satisfaction and life fulfillment.

If you really want it, you can do it! I believe in you. Now you must, too.

Best wishes. Happy organizing!

Sara Pedersen,
Professional Organizer & Career Coach

P.S. If you'd like a little one-on-one coaching via phone or email, please just call me at 651/717-1284 to schedule a Phone Coaching Session. We can discuss your specific questions and needs to get your business off to a great start.

also available from Time to Organize

IN-PERSON, PHONE, AND EMAIL COACHING SESSIONS

- Working with your first clients, challenges, expectations, and solutions
- Other custom-designed coaching sessions – just ask!

READY-TO-USE EDITABLE WORD OR PDF CLIENT FORMS

- Client Phone Intake Form
- Client Assessment Form (Comprehensive Version)
- Client Service Agreement Form
- Client Action Plan Form
- Client Feedback Survey

LEARN TO ORGANIZE BOOK

- This book is the companion to the Born to Organize career guide. Learn step by step how to organize simple spaces like entryways and bathrooms; discover new storage methods for complex areas like kitchens and craft areas; get a handle on paper clutter, filing, and photos; set up a handy household command center; and more.

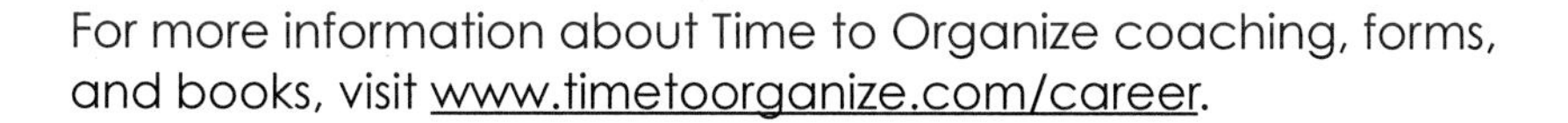
For more information about Time to Organize coaching, forms, and books, visit www.timetoorganize.com/career.

MARKETING & BUSINESS DEVELOPMENT PRODUCTS

- Articles on Demand: Using Articles on Demand™ is easy! Simply browse our vast online selection of organizing-themed articles, place your order via credit card, and we'll email you the article. Then copy and paste the text into your own marketing materials. Filled with helpful organizing tips and techniques, the articles are both educational and entertaining.

- Girls' Night Out Organizing Workshop Kits: If you're looking for another income stream in addition to hands-on organizing, hosting a Girls' Night Out Organizing Workshop may be just the thing to add to your repertoire of services! Everything you need to market, prepare for, and hold Girls' Night Out Organizing Workshops is included in your purchase.

- Marketing Tip Sheets: Choose from Pinterest for Small Business Owners How-To Guide, Facebook for Small Business Owners How-To Guide, Purposeful Website Planning How-To Guide, 50 Bright Ideas to Market Your Small Business Tip Sheet, and Publicity Rocks! How-To Guide.

- Facebook Posts on Demand: Thanks to Posts on Demand, you can have a year's worth of Facebook posts right at your fingertips! This unique subscription service lets you showcase your expertise, get the online conversation started, and educate and entertain your fans.

For more information about Time to Organize marketing products, visit: www.timetoorganize.com/marketing.

inspiring words

Find a need and fill it.
— Ruth Stafford Peale

He who does not get fun and enjoyment out of everyday… needs to reorganize his life.
— George Matthew Adams

The great thing to learn about life is, first, not to do what you don't want to do, and second, to do what you do want to do.
— Margaret Anderson

Find out what you like doing best and get someone to pay you for doing it.
— Katharine Whitehorn

In order to be irreplaceable one must always be different.
— Coco Chanel

It's the moment you think you can't that you realize you can.
— Celine Dion

Work... has always been my favorite form of recreation.
— Anna Howard Shaw

about the author

"Anything is easy when you know how to do it." That's advice Sara Pedersen received from her grandfather many years ago. With the help of those encouraging words, she founded Time to Organize LLC in 2000. After years of teaching Twin Cities residents to organize, simplify, and discover time to do the things they love, she now shares her knowledge with prospective and new professional organizers as a career coach. She is able to teach them "how to do it," making it easy to launch new, successful careers as professional organizers.

Sara has a B.A. in journalism from the University of Minnesota. She has worked in print production, project management, and marketing communications roles, and she currently uses those skills by offering marketing services and products for small business owners.

Sara is an active member of the National Association of Productivity and Organizing Professionals (NAPO). She has held the positions of Secretary, Newsletter Editor, Public Relations Director, and Electronic Communications Chair for NAPO-MN. She is also currently an Ambassador for NAPO at a national level and a member of the elite Golden Circle of NAPO for veteran professional organizers.

Contact Sara at Time to Organize if you'd like to learn more about organizing as a career.

phone: 651-717-1284
email: sara@timetoorganize.com
website: www.timetoorganize.com

PLEASE CONNECT WITH SARA VIA SOCIAL MEDIA AS WELL:

facebook: www.facebook.com/timetoorganize
twitter: www.twitter.com/SaraPedersen
linkedin: www.linkedin.com/in/sarapedersen
pinterest: www.pinterest.com/saraped